3 1994 00940 7161

SANTA ANA PUBLIC LIBRARY

D0859599

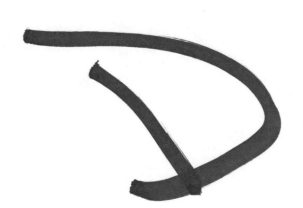

20th Century Sports

Images of Greatness

796.0973 MES
Meserole, Mike
20th century sports

$26.95
CENTRAL   31994009407161

Copyright © 1999 Total/SPORTS ILLUSTRATED

All rights reserved.

No part of this book may be reproduced or transmitted in any form or by any means, electronic or mechanical, including photocopying, recording, or by any information storage and retrieval system, without permission in writing from the publisher.

Total/SPORTS ILLUSTRATED is a trademark of Time Inc.
Used under license.

For information about permission to reproduce selections from this book, please write to:
Permissions
Total/SPORTS ILLUSTRATED
100 Enterprise Drive
Kingston, New York 12401

Visit www.totalsports.net and www.cnnsi.com

Permissions appear on pages 255–256.

A conscientious attempt has been made to contact proprietors of the rights in every image used in the book. If through inadvertence the publisher has failed to identify any holder of rights, forgiveness is requested and corrected information will be entered in future printings.

BOOK DESIGN BY BARBARA MARKS

ISBN: 1-892129-12-4

Library of Congress Catalog Card Number: 99-63223

Printed in United States of America

2 4 6 8 10 9 7 5 3 1

Acknowledgments

This is a family album of the twentieth century, the great extended family of sport. The century opens with the primitive fun and games of young America at play and a world united, if only for a while, by a revived Olympic ideal; it closes five generations later with sports firmly rooted as a national and international obsession. As with any collection of family photos, a few favorite moments and personalities are bound to be missing, but their absence is eased by an abundance of previously unseen images that reflect the flavor and athletic intensity of each decade.

The blueprint for *20th Century Sports* was rolled out by Total Sports publisher John Thorn and has been wonderfully realized by designer Barbara Marks. Project editor Beau Riffenburgh kept everyone's eye on the ball and production coordinator Donna Harris was, as usual, indispensable. Photo editor Mark Rucker unearthed countless rarities and plumbed a multitude of sports-photo sources. Stanley Weil of *Sports Illustrated* also helped to shape this first major publication under the joint imprint of Total/*Sports Illustrated*. Robert W. Creamer graced the volume with a splendid introduction.

Gathering photographs was a herculean task made easier with the assistance of John Blackmar and Ted Menzis of *Sports Illustrated;* Joanna Keating of AP/Wide World Photos; and Kristine Hook and James Lance at Corbis Images.

Additional help in acquiring photos was provided by: Bill Burdick of the National Baseball Library; Carol Butler of Brown Brothers; Craig Campbell of the Hockey Hall of Fame; Liz Gray of the *Pittsburgh Post-Gazette;* Preston Levi of the International Swimming Hall of Fame; Chuck Rand of the National Cowboy Hall of Fame; Allen Reuben of Culver Photos; Phyllis Rogers of Keeneland Association; Peter Rohowsky of Archive Photos; Leith Rohr of the Chicago Historical Society; Michael Salmon of the Amateur Athletic Foundation; Suzanne Simmons of Allsport Photography; Kelli Souder at Time Life Syndication; Doug Stark of the Naismith Memorial Basketball Hall of Fame; Paul Spinelli of NFL Properties; Kent Stephens of the College Football Hall of Fame; Richard L. Tritt of the Cumberland County (Pa.) Historical Society; and Maxine Vigliotta of the U.S. Golf Association.

Research assistance was provided by Liz Cruwys of the Scott Polar Research Institute; Dan Diamond of Dan Diamond & Associates; Dick Hamilton of the National Museum of Racing Hall of Fame; Buzz McKim of Daytona International Speedway; John Wilcockson, editor of *VeloNews;* and Ken Thomas.

Total Sports would also like to thank Jimmy Biedrzycki and Gene Stuttman of Coral Graphics, Brad Gill of PBM Graphics Inc., and Michele Rothfarb and Kevin Rafferty of Quebecor World.

Finally, this project could not have been completed without the aid and support of the dedicated publishing crew in Kingston, New York, mainly, Ann Sullivan, Jed Thorn, Bob Hueber, Chad Lawrence, Ben Campbell, Darryl Litts, Matt Silverman, Connie Neuhauser, and Pat Shaw.

MIKE MESEROLE
September 1999

Contents

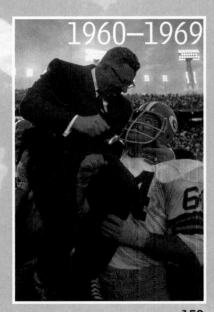

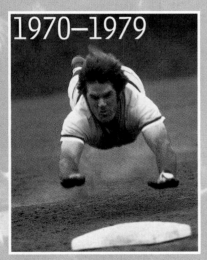

Foreword

Robert W. Creamer

The question is: can photography be art? More to the point, can sports photography be art?

Before photography came along, painting for most artists was a job, a livelihood. Geniuses took art beyond that, of course, but most people toiling with easel and brush were working stiffs, hacks trying to earn a living by reproducing as best they could a face or, rarely, a familiar scene, and hoping they'd come up with something that would be close enough to reality to sell.

According to one definition, art is "an attempt to capture time, to hold it still," and that's pretty much what workaday artists were trying to do for their clients. When photography arrived in the first half of the nineteenth century, many thought it meant the end of art as they knew it. No matter how skillful you were with paint or pencil, why bother if you could recreate a face or a scene with a camera?

Great artists disagreed. James McNeill Whistler, the vain, petulant American genius, said, "If a man who paints only the tree, or flower or other surface he sees before him were an artist, the king of artists would be the photographer. It is for the artist to do something beyond this: in portrait painting to put on canvas something more than the face the model wears for that one day, to paint the man, in short, as well as his features."

Whistler's comment was snide and shortsighted in view of what photography later accomplished, but you can understand what he meant. In the Frick Collection on Fifth Avenue in New York City there's a room with a number of portraits of upper-class English women during the reign of King George III

(1760–1820). The paintings are technically superb, rich in color and detail, reproducing not just the faces but the silks and laces of their dresses, kerchiefs, and caps. But the portraits, except for one, tend to merge into a sameness, an almost monotonous repetition of supercilious and not very attractive women in beautiful clothes.

The one exception jumps off the wall at you. The painting seems alive. The eyes glow, there's a little half-smile, an amused but seductive glance. You want to know more about this woman. You wish you could meet her. You look at the nameplate and discover it's a portrait by George Romney of Emma Hamilton, the low-born gamine who, despite her proletarian speech and manners and, later, her sloppy obesity, charmed and slept her way to the highest circles of English society, marrying a nobleman's son and becoming the mistress of England's heroic admiral, Horatio Nelson. Look at the portrait in the Frick, and you suddenly understand why. You feel her charm. I mean, you fall in love with the woman, and you know why Sir William Hamilton and Admiral Nelson were hooked. To recall Whistler, there's a lot more in the painting than the face Emma Hamilton wore to the studio that day. Romney, who was in love with her too, captured the essence of the woman.

Can photography, so casually disparaged by Whistler, do that? Turn to the opening spread of the chapter on the 1920–29 decade and look at the extraordinary photograph of Hack Wilson, who hit 56 home runs for the Chicago Cubs nearly 70 years ago. It's not a portrait in the posed sense because it's a moment of violent action, and it's not important for being a record of a signal moment in baseball history—Wilson appears to have swung and missed—but it doesn't matter. What the photo says is: *this* is Hack Wilson, and once you see it you never forget him.

It's an action photo, yet what a portrait! What a delineation of this strange, foreshortened, powerful little man, committing everything he has into the swing of the bat, into this one thing he did so well. So much for James McNeill Whistler; I can't imagine a painting of a batter capturing the same emotion this photograph does. You don't have to be a sports fan or know who Wilson was or what he did to savor the picture. It grabs you, as Emma Hamilton's portrait does. It becomes part of your cultural baggage.

Sports photography does that. A great and admirable part of it is the memory-stirring recording of superb athletes and classic moments (Red Grange moving downfield, Gordie Howe riding an opponent into the boards, Roger Bannister running the first four-minute mile), but it does wonderful things with less obvious subjects as well.

There are Philistines among us who believe that what goes on in the air above second base during the execution of a double play is as graceful and beautiful as anything that occurs on stage during a classical ballet; we are grateful to sports photography for being able to stop that motion in midair and show us we are right. The sports photographer can do that because sports photography has always been at the cutting edge of technology, and sometimes ahead of it, as the practitioners of the craft (all art begins with craft) seek faster film, longer lenses, motorized equipment, new lab techniques, anything that will help them get further inside, close up, right to the nub of what's going on. The surface brutality of football masks the subtle skills of the game, the amazing grace

under pressure (where else could that tired phrase be better applied?) of a quarterback, about to be run over by a 275-pound lineman, who stands in and holds his ground to gain a precious nanosecond before throwing the ball to the now open pass receiver at just the right moment. The best in the business, such as Walter Iooss and Neil Leifer and their disciples, know how to find such moments and take us into them.

The technology is important, and has been since Joseph Nicéphore Niepce produced his first negative. The primitive equipment constructed by John D. Isaacs in the 1870s to photograph horses in action had a shutter speed of 1/2000 of a second and in a sense was the direct ancestor of the sophisticated gear even rank amateurs are familiar with today. Sports photographers down the years have leaped on new developments: flash powder, Speed Graphics, light meters, Big Berthas, 35-mm "candid cameras," single-lens reflexes, fish-eye lenses, super-fast film, power-driven shutter speeds. . . . It goes on and on.

Yet it's more than technology. Technology in itself can be self-defeating, with the gimmick getting ahead of the result. The following may betray more of my Philistinism, but I might as well confess a disenchantment with the remarkable outdoor vistas produced by the acclaimed photographic artists Edward Weston and Ansel Adams. Their museum-collection masterpieces were created to a considerable degree by the extraordinary technical command they held over aspects of photography ranging from special filters to unique lenses to odd methods of developing prints. Admirable, but for me the classic beauty of their photographs has a cold, lifeless sterility, like a Martian landscape. I turn to the work of, say, Henri Cartier-Bresson and Roy de Carava and feel life pouring back into the scene. Cartier-Bresson and de Carava certainly take advantage of technological advances, but their cameras seek out evidence of the presence of men and women rather than their absence, of life rather than sterility. Weston and Adams put great store in what they did with their film after they took the picture, but Edward Steichen, the American who helped so much to move photography toward fine art, had a different opinion. "When that shutter clicks," he said, "anything else that can be done afterward is not worth consideration." Cartier-Bresson, in saluting an older photographer he had learned from, said, "He made me realize that photographs could reach eternity through the moment."

The moment. Isn't that what sports photography is primarily about?

Technology is fine, but it can be overdone. "You don't send an assault team out to capture a delicate emotion," said W. Eugene Smith of *Life* magazine. The ultimate technology is in the eye and hands of the photographer. It's sobering to realize that for all the modern advances in the field there has never been a sports action photo more dramatic or exciting than the one in this book from the early years of the century of Ty Cobb ferociously and efficiently sliding into third base under Jimmy Austin's leaping legs. The paradox is: the more powerful the telephoto lens, the farther the photographer is from the subject. Maybe that doesn't matter, but an uneasy feeling says it does.

The camera is the sports photographer's easel and brush but it's what he or she does with it that creates the art. Luck enters into it, too, since some of the greatest photographs are the result of an accident of timing, although it's what you do with luck that counts. Branch Rickey's oft-quoted adage, "Luck is the residue of design," makes it clear that, as another sports maxim has it, "Good teams make their own

luck." The best photographers, like the best teams, are ready when the unexpected happens.

The critic Michael Wood quotes a passage from a poem by W. H. Auden that says, "The crow on the crematorium chimney/And the camera roving the battle/Record a space where time has no place." The camera for Auden "becomes the means not of freezing time, but of marking the silent specificity of the passing moment."

That's pretty good. "Time has no place"— timelessness. Don Larsen's perfect game is 40 years past but Larsen on the mound and Yogi Berra leaping into his arms still are now. In the Hack Wilson portrait and in the shot of Ty Cobb sliding, the "specificity of the passing moment" is the essence of almost inexpressible effort. Albert Einstein when he was messing around with problems of space and time said, "A photograph never grows old." Auden and Einstein understood what photography could do, and their definitions fit sports photography perfectly. Time has raced relentlessly ahead since the camera caught Michael Jordan draining his last, game-winning, championship-winning jumper, but time has no place in that space now. The specificity of the fabulous, passing moment, captured by the sports photographer's camera, doesn't grow old.

Look at the picture of Man o' War in full flight, miles ahead of the Triple Crown winner Sir Barton, breezing to victory in the final race of his career in a runaway presaging that of Secretariat in the Belmont half a century later. Those of us who never saw Man o' War run, which means most of us, can sense, looking at the photograph, what that fabulous racehorse meant to those who did see him. You can feel the strength, the drive, the urgency, the grace, the flow. You feel the emotion he created. I'm sorry to keep ragging Whistler, but no painting of a racehorse can

begin to convey the feeling stirred by such a photograph. For that matter, very few paintings have been able to capture sport the way photography has. I can think of Thomas Eakins' scullers and George Bellows' boxers and not a lot more. Edgar Degas, a nonathlete famous for his portrayals of ballet dancers, "had a passion for painting living forms in motion" and spent a lot of time at the racetrack doing horses. But Degas usually did them before or after racing, and there's no action that comes close to the splendor of the Man o' War photo. It's too bad that when Degas visited America—he had relatives in New Orleans—he didn't find his way to a baseball park, although I doubt that even he could have done justice to a second baseman on the pivot. Photography is the art of sport.

It's pleasant to note that photography was officially born in the summer of 1839, the same year legend says baseball, America's first big-ticket sport, was invented by Abner Doubleday in Cooperstown, New York. We know now that baseball in one form or another had been played for half a century and more before Doubleday laid out his mythical diamond, and that the rules of our modern game weren't set down until six years after Abner's

supposed brainstorm. And photography had existed in rudimentary and experimental forms for decades before the procedures devised jointly by Niepce and Louis Jacques Daguerre were announced to the world on August 19, 1839.

Nonetheless, it's nice to know that photography and big-time sport arrived hand in hand, so to speak, even if it did take decades for America to become preoccupied with games and for photography to record that preoccupation. The urgencies of sport pushed photography to extend itself; it's obvious that sport contributed greatly to the expansion of photography as an art. And photography, in synergistic response, certainly enhanced sport, opening the world's eyes to its beauty and possibilities.

Finally, it's fun to report an appealing coincidence. The first issue of *Sports Illustrated*, dated August 16, 1954, appeared exactly 115 years to the week after the announcement of photography's birth. Now there's synergy for you. Sports magazines and books like this one could not exist without photography, and photography has had much of its most brilliant expression in their pages. Come and see. 🐚

20th Century Sports

1900–1909

Pregame scene, 1903 World Series, Boston

1900–1909

The United States had

become a world power in 1898 by winning the Spanish-American War in just 113 days and on two fronts—in the Caribbean and the Pacific. Not even the shock of President McKinley's assassination in 1901 could dent the nation's confidence in its prospects for the twentieth century. And no American radiated more confidence than McKinley's young successor, Theodore Roosevelt, a former Harvard boxer, cattle rancher, explorer, and war hero, whom sporting goods king A.G. Spalding called "our first athletic President." Roosevelt believed sport molded character and preached that, "in life, as in a football game, the principle to follow is: don't foul and don't shirk, but hit the line hard." ❧ **In the fall of 1905,** Roosevelt mediated the peace conference that ended the Russo-Japanese War, a diplomatic feat that would earn him the Nobel Peace Prize. He then turned his attention to the battlefields of college football where, during the previous season alone, lethal variations of the old flying wedge and equally brutal defensive countermeasures had combined to kill 18 players and seriously injure 149 others. Summoning several leaders of the game to the White House, Roosevelt voiced the public's outrage at such organized mayhem and demanded that the sport be made safe or he would abolish it. ❧ **Later that year,** representatives of 62 colleges met in New York to form the Intercollegiate Athletic Association of the United States (IAAUS). Moving quickly, the new football rules committee outlawed all mass-momentum plays, approved the forward pass, established a one-yard neutral zone at the line of scrimmage and increased first-down yardage to 10 yards. Later changes would add a fourth down, increase the value of a touchdown to six points, and decrease the points for a field goal to three. While

1900

MAY 11
Heavyweight champion Jim Jeffries knocks out former champion James J. (Gentleman Jim) Corbett in 23rd round of their title bout at Coney Island, N.Y.

AUG. 10
United States defeats British Isles, 3–0, in first Davis Cup tennis matches at Longwood Cricket Club near Boston.

OCT. 28
Second modern Olympic Games, held in conjunction with Paris World's Fair, conclude with United States team of 55 college and club athletes dominating track and field events with 53 medals.

1901

JAN. 11
First National Bowling Championships held in Chicago and sanctioned by the American Bowling Congress.

FEB. 27
National League Rules Committee announces that henceforth all foul balls will count as strikes, except after two strikes.

APRIL 24
American League (formerly Western Association) debuts with Chicago White Stockings defeating Cleveland Blues, 8–2, at South Side Park.

OCT. 4
Columbia beats British challenger *Shamrock II* in three straight races off Newport, Rhode Island, as a United States yacht successfully defends the America's Cup for the 11th straight time since 1870.

1902

JAN. 1
Unbeaten Michigan routs Stanford, 49–0, in first Rose Bowl game at Pasadena, Calif. The "Point-a-Minute" Wolverines end 1901 season scoring 550 points and giving up none.

AUG. 8
United States wins second Davis Cup matches with 3–2 victory over British Isles in Brooklyn, N.Y.

Moleskin pants and leather helmets (if any)

SEPT. 28
American League ends second season outdrawing older National League in attendance, 2,206,454 paying customers to 1,683,012.

1903

JAN. 9
American League president Ban Johnson rejects National League offer to merge into one 12-team major league. AL also votes to move Baltimore franchise to New York.

AUG. 8
United States loses possession of Davis Cup for first time, dropping 4–1 decision to brothers Laurie and Reggie Doherty of British Isles.

OCT. 13
American League champion Boston Pilgrims defeat pennant-winning Pittsburgh Pirates of the National League, five games to three, in first World Series.

SEPT. 2
U.S. yacht *Reliance* successfully defends America's Cup, beating Britain's *Shamrock III* in three straight races.

1904

JAN. 28
Frank Gotch beats champion Tom Jenkins to win catch-as-catch-can heavyweight wrestling championship in Bellingham, Wash.

FEB. 22
National Ski Association of America is founded in Ishpeming, Mich.

OCT. 10
Baseball's regular season ends with Boston Pilgrims (AL) and New York Giants (NL) as pennant winners, but second World Series is cancelled when Giants' manager John McGraw and owner John T. Brush refuse to play champions of what they consider to be a minor league.

NOV. 23
Third Olympiad of modern era, which is held as part of St. Louis World's Fair, comes to a close. With most European countries skipping Games, American athletes win 244 out of 281 medals.

Willie Hoppe won his first balkline championship in 1906 and was still three-cushion champ in 1952.

casualties continued to mount through 1909, the new rules succeeded in opening up the game by emphasizing speed and movement in the quest for touchdowns rather than kicking position. In 1910, the IAAUS changed its name to the National Collegiate Athletic Association. ❧ The amateur status of student-athletes was another problem facing the IAAUS, although the sport that concerned administrators this time was baseball rather than football. While professional football was in its infancy in the early 1900s and confined mainly to Ohio and Pennsylvania, pro baseball had two eight-team major leagues and sold millions of tickets every year. There were also a growing number of minor league and semi-pro teams with rosters to fill in the summer months when college ballplayers were on vacation and looking to earn a few dollars before classes resumed in the fall. The issue came down to this: should a student who accepts money to play summer ball be considered a professional, and, if so, should he forfeit his amateur eligibility? Unlike football reform, the summer baseball question generated protracted debate and was not resolved until 1916, when the NCAA officially defined an amateur athlete as one who "participates in competitive physical sports only for the pleasure and the physical, mental, moral, and social benefits directly derived therefrom." ❧ That fell in line with the International Olympic

American shootists, 1908 Olympics

Committee's view that an amateur athlete engaged in sports only as a pastime, not a profession. Such a definition, of course, separated the lower classes from the leisure class, which could afford to train and compete without material benefit. ❧ **The ancient games of Greece** had been revived after a lapse of 15 centuries in 1894 under the leadership of French aristocrat and educator Baron Pierre de Coubertin, who hoped to promote international fair play and good sportsmanship through athletic competition. The first modern Olympic Games were held in Athens two years later, attended by 311 athletes from 12 nations and financed by a donation of one million drachmas from Greek philanthropist Georgios Averoff and by the sale of souvenir stamps and medals. Although the United States sent no official team, 13 Americans, mostly college kids and members of the Boston Athletic Association, won 11 championships, including nine of the 12 track and field events. ❧ **The second and third Olympics** were staged during the World's Fairs of Paris in 1900 and St. Louis in 1904 and were largely ignored. The U.S. dominated the St. Louis Games, winning 23 of 25 track and field events and 80 percent of the medals overall, but only 10 other nations sent teams. Four years later in London, 20 countries showed up and the Yanks still won 15 of 26 events. ❧ **As more and more Americans** began to participate in sports at the turn of the century, the wealthy tended to concentrate on pursuits

1905

MAY 13
Jim Jeffries retires as undefeated world heavyweight champion, then referees July 3 fight between Marvin Hart and Jack Root in Reno to determine his successor. Hart knocks out Root in 12th round.

JULY 8
Eighteen-year-old American May Sutton becomes first overseas player—man or woman—to win Wimbledon singles title, beating defending champion Dorothea Douglass.

OCT. 7
Dan Patch lowers world pacing record for one mile to 1:55 1/2 at Red Mile course in Lexington, Ky. Mark will stand for 33 years.

OCT. 14
New York Giants, who now approve of World Series, win second championship between two leagues, four games to one, over Philadelphia Athletics. Giants' pitcher Christy Mathewson tosses three shutouts and scatters 14 hits.

NOV. 30
University of Chicago upsets visiting Michigan, 2–0, on Thanksgiving to end Wolverines' five-year, 56-game unbeaten streak.

DEC. 28
Representatives of 62 colleges and universities meet in New York to reform college football and establish Intercollegiate Athletic Association of the United States (IAAUS).

1906

FEB. 23
Canadian challenger Tommy Burns wins world heavyweight title in 20-round decision over champion Marvin Hart in Los Angeles.

MAY 2
After unsuccessful Olympiads in 1900 and 1904, Athens celebrates 10th anniversary of modern Olympics with completion of the unofficial "Intercalated Games." These interim Olympics are attended by 20 nations and help revive the movement.

MAY 23
Frank Gotch regains world catch-as-catch-can wrestling title, defeating champion Tom Jenkins in two straight falls.

SEPTEMBER
College football season begins with rules changes legalizing forward pass and requiring 10 yards for first down.

OCT. 14
Chicago White Sox, nicknamed the "Hitless Wonders" after taking AL pennant with team batting average of .230, hit just .196 in World Series but beat cross-town Cubs, four games to two.

NOV. 28
World lightweight champion "Philadelphia Jack" O'Brien fights heavyweight champ Tommy Burns to 20-round draw.

APRIL 19
Canada's Tom Longboat wins 11th running of Boston Marathon in 2:24:20, lowering course record by over five minutes.

OCT. 12
Chicago Cubs complete first World Series four-game sweep over Detroit Tigers, after first game ends in 3–3 tie after 12 innings.

1907

OCT. 12
Two sisters meet in final of U.S. Women's Amateur golf championship match for the only time this century as Margaret Curtis defeats defending champion Harriot Curtis, 7 and 6.

NOVEMBER
At National Horse Show in New York, Mrs. J. Marion Edmonds becomes first woman to ride astride a horse in competition.

1908

JULY 24
Runner-up John Hayes of U.S. is declared winner of marathon at London Olympic Games after Americans protest that British officials helped exhausted Italian runner Dorando Pietri across finish line. Great Britain wins most medals but U.S. athletes, as usual, dominate track and field.

George Hackenschmidt (left) in a 1908 tuneup for his championship match with Frank Gotch

beyond the reach of the public, like tennis, golf, polo, and yachting. In fact, the U.S. Lawn Tennis Championships and the America's Cup yacht races were both centered in the summer playground of the Eastern elite, Newport, Rhode Island. The common man enjoyed watching bicycle races, billiard matches, and the catch-as-catch-can, or freestyle, wrestling of Tom Jenkins, Frank Gotch, and George Hackenschmidt. The traveling Wild West re-enactment shows of "Buffalo Bill" Cody and trick shot artist Annie Oakley were also popular, both in the U.S. and Europe. ✒ **Major League Baseball,** which consisted of just the National League at the turn of the century, was held in the same low esteem by the American public as college football. Greedy owners, grousing players, dirty play, rowdy fans, and a lack of competitive teams were threatening to ruin the game. That changed in 1901, when American League president Ban Johnson challenged the 24-year-old National League with his new circuit of eight teams and began raiding NL rosters. Offering players more money and fans lower ticket prices, Johnson also promised to clean up the game on the field and in the grandstands. Within two years the new league had more star players—like Cy Young, Nap Lajoie, and Ed Delahanty—and a half million more paying customers. In 1903, the National League decided to cut its losses and make peace with the upstarts. The truce called for both leagues to respect each other's contracts and reserve clauses and agree to a three-man commission to govern the game. Johnson's was the commission's most powerful voice. ✒ **The most exciting byproduct of the peace** came at the end of the season when the AL champion Boston Pilgrims accepted the challenge of the NL champion Pittsburgh Pirates to play a best-of-nine-games "World Series." Boston won, five games to three, and a tradition was born. 🐿

With peace on the field and the World Series to look forward to each fall,

baseball's popularity soared after 1905. New heroes emerged, from the hot-tempered, win-at-all-costs Ty Cobb in Detroit to the New York Giants' clean-cut Christy Mathewson, who was the embodiment of the dashing Frank Merriwell figure of the dime novels. And then there was Rube Waddell of the Philadelphia A's, an eccentric left-hander who led the AL in strikeouts for six straight seasons. The Rube was as ignorant as Matty was cultured, and as guileless as Cobb was nasty. He wasn't a roughneck and he wasn't a saint; he was something else: a character. And baseball fans couldn't get enough of him. 🐿

Meanwhile, another original was causing a sensation in boxing. Jack

Johnson was the heavyweight champion of the world and he was black, a fact that most white American fight fans were reluctant to accept and for which Johnson wasn't about to apologize. The son of a former slave, he proved himself first in so-called "battle royals" where several black fighters would enter the ring together and fight to the finish for the amusement of white audiences. He won the black heavyweight title in 1903 then had to wait five years before getting a shot at the world championship, taking the title from Tommy Burns by knockout.

🐿 **In 1907 President Roosevelt** sent 16 battleships, all painted white, on a goodwill tour around the globe to demonstrate the American naval power behind his "big stick" foreign policy. Dubbed "the Great White Fleet," the armada returned 14 months later, just as boxing writers were pleading with former heavyweight champion Jim Jeffries to come out of retirement and take on Johnson. They called Jeffries "the Great White Hope." 🐿

AUG 25
Allen Winter wins $30,000 first prize before crowd of 20,000 at first American Trotting Derby in Readville, Mass.

SEPT. 23
Fred Merkle's controversial base-running mistake with two outs in bottom of ninth inning against Chicago Cubs at Polo Grounds winds up costing New York Giants National League pennant. Merkle, aboard at first base, failed to touch second when winning run was singled in from third. Game is replayed after completion of season when Giants and Cubs tie for first place. Cubs win replay and flag.

OCT. 14
Chicago Cubs repeat as World Series champions, eliminating Detroit in five games.

DEC. 26
Jack Johnson becomes first black fighter to win world heavyweight title, when he defeats champion Tommy Burns by TKO in 14 rounds at Sydney, Australia.

1909

APRIL 12
Philadelphia's Shibe Park, baseball's first steel-and-concrete stadium, attracts major league-record 31,160 fans as Athletics defeat Boston Red Sox, 8–1.

JUNE 29
A Ford wins first transcontinental auto race from Washington, D.C., to Seattle.

JULY 19
National League president Harry Pulliam, suffering from bad health and job problems, dies of self-inflicted gunshot wound.

OCT. 16
Detroit Tigers lose third straight World Series, this time in seven games, to Pittsburgh Pirates.

DEC. 4
Pacer Dan Patch, holder of nine world records, is retired at age 13 following racing career that included 30 sub-two-minute miles.

Rube Waddell, sensational "sousepaw," 1902

Four great fighters: Joe Walcott (left) and Joe Gans squared off for a 20-round draw in San Francisco, September 30, 1904. (Bottom) Jack Johnson KO'd Stanley Ketchel in the 12th round, October 16, 1909; Ketchel, giving away 35 pounds, had flattened Johnson earlier in the round.

Aquatic competition at the Olympics: (above) the Swedish team showing off at the 1908 games in London; (right) the "swimmin' hole" start of the 100-meter freestyle at St. Louis in 1904; Zoltan de Halmay of Hungary won the event.

Few nations had sent athletes to the first two Olympiads, so the entrance of these two Zulu tribesmen, Lentauw and Yamasani, in the marathon at the 1904 Games was a delight.

The highlight of the London Games was the marathon, in which a dazed Dorando Pietri was half-dragged to victory. He was later disqualified in favor of Johnny Hayes (U.S.).

Speed with style:
the yacht *Columbia*
defeated England's
Shamrock II to win the
America's Cup in 1901.

One year later,
Henry Ford posed
with his Ford Racer
999, Barney Oldfield
at the wheel.

You've come a long way, baby. This image and the one below portray a gentler age for sports, if a more constricting one for women.

Wood skis are rarely seen today, but their devotees swear by them.

Women began to play golf in the U.S. in 1891 at the Shinnecock Hills Club on Long Island, where two years later the club provided a nine-hole course for their sole use. Before the century's turn, women had USGA-sanctioned tournaments of their own, too.

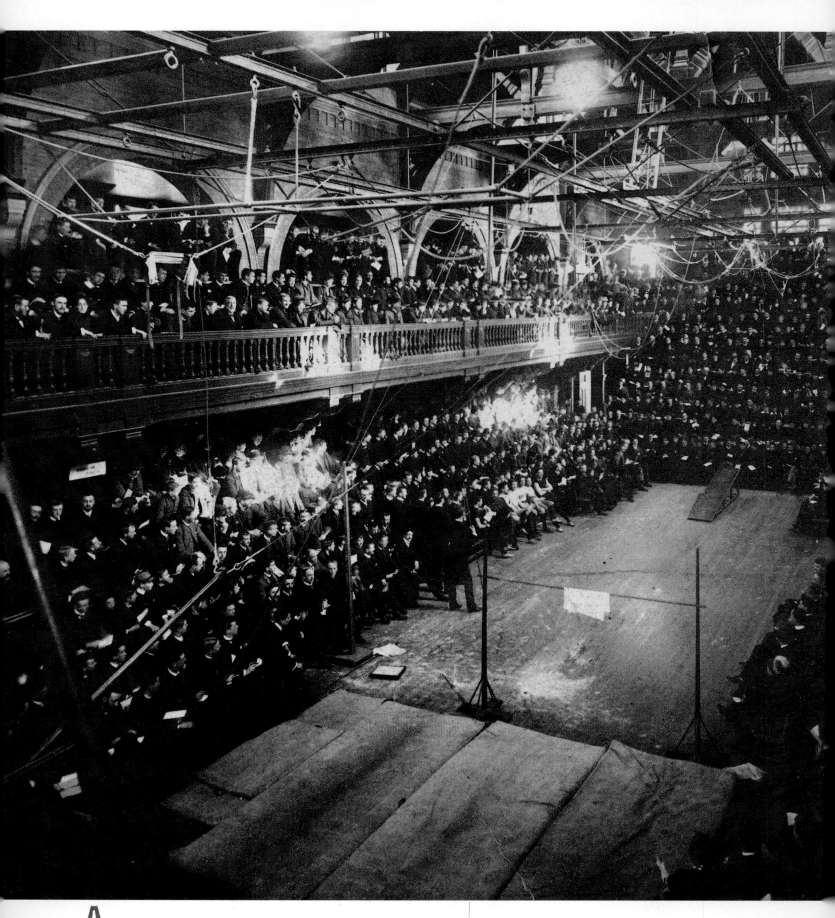

A gymnastics meet was the epitome of athleticism between the 1840s and the First World War, when the German *turnverein* movement swept America. Social and sport clubs dedicated to physical fitness, the *turnverein* movement and its "turners," or gymnasts, gave rise to participatory sport.

Turn-of-the-century swingers: (above) the advent of loose-fitting garb like bloomers and the sailor's blouse enabled women to extend their reach past the "refined" lawn sports into real muscularity; (left) J.D. Harris, medal-bedecked Indian-club twirler.

Invented in 1891 by Canadian James Naismith at the Springfield, Massachusetts, YMCA, basketball was the first purely North American sport since lacrosse. Instantly popular as indoor recreation for the winter months, as played at Columbia University (right), it had an air of novelty that inspired innovation. If one could play water polo, after all, why not equestrian basketball?

In 1910, when pallor was beautiful and facility in fainting a mark of refinement, James Sullivan, chairman of the Amateur Athletic Union, argued that interscholastic athletics for females was a "spectacle" best to be avoided. A decade later, *The New York Times* reported on a basketball game: "Are there any obstacles other than convention and tradition in the way of intercollegiate sports for women? It is difficult to imagine them. This is the day of the girl athlete and, sooner or later, she is bound to assert herself to obtain full freedom for college competitions."

Football injuries of a horrific nature—including on-field fatalities—were a product of mass-momentum plays like the flying wedge and of the mayhem that went with rugby-like scrums. By mid-decade, rules-makers separated the combatants at the line of scrimmage by creating a neutral zone, limited the number of men in the backfield to four, and outlawed mass plays and linked blocking.

Members of Robert Falcon Scott's first Antarctic expedition, 1901–04, engage in what surely was the first soccer game ever played on the continent.

From 1898 until 1910 a football field was marked with lines parallel to the sidelines to help ensure that the line of scrimmage was crossed at least five yards from where the ball had been put into play—whence the vestigial term "gridiron."

Christy Mathewson was the darling of the New York press and hero to right-thinking children everywhere. Apart from being a model of moral rectitude, Matty was a football All-America, a champion checkers player, and a heckuva pitcher for the New York Giants.

They didn't name the award for best pitcher after this guy for nothing. In 22 years in the big leagues, Cy Young won a staggering total of 511 games. Here he is, fat and 40 but still in his prime, ca. 1908.

A spillover crowd at New York's Polo Grounds watches a thrilling one-game playoff to break a season-ending tie for the 1908 National League pennant. Alas for the hometown fans, the Giants and Christy Mathewson lost to Three Finger Brown of the Chicago Cubs, 4–2.

Poor Fred Merkle. Had he touched second base on September 23, 1908, rather than veering toward the clubhouse, there would have been no need for the playoff game (left). But "Merkle's Boner" transformed a teammate's single into a forceout, a win into a tie, and his name into an epithet.

1910–1919

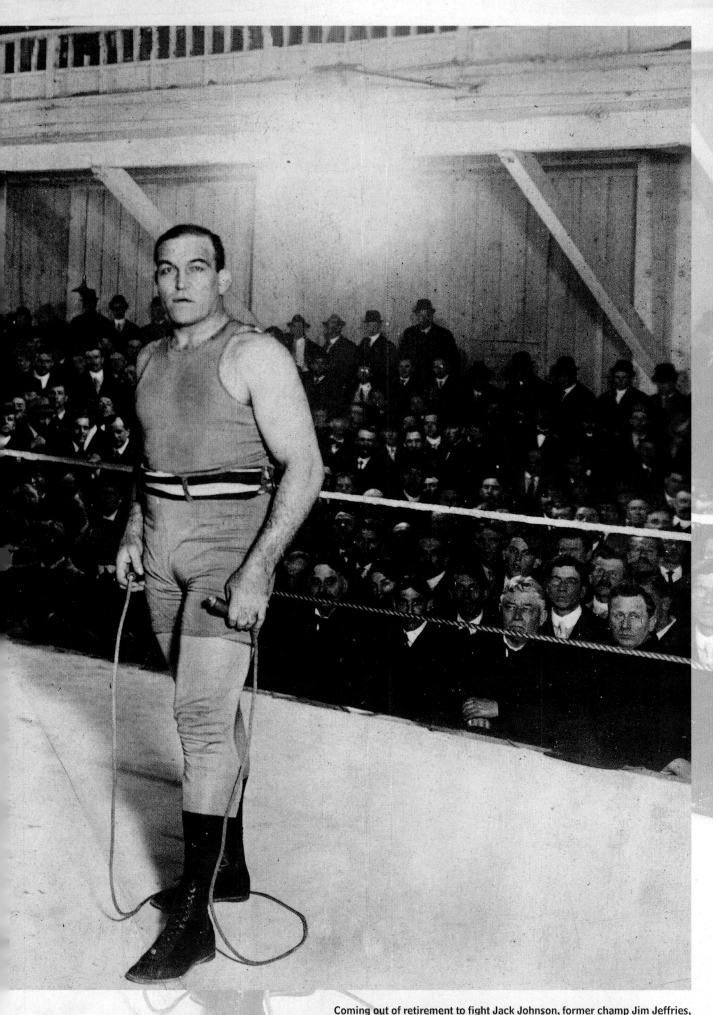

Coming out of retirement to fight Jack Johnson, former champ Jim Jeffries, "the Great White Hope," works himself back into shape.

1910–1919

George Lewis "Tex"

Rickard liked to take his chances. An orphan at 10, he worked cattle drives from Texas to Montana as a teenager, was a town marshal at 21, then set out for Alaska in 1895 to dig for gold. In the next eight years, he made and lost two fortunes in the Klondike gold rush and ran gambling saloons in Dawson and Nome. In 1903 he followed his fellow prospectors to Goldfield, Nevada, and built another casino there. **Eager to put Goldfield on the map** and mindful that nothing drew the attention of high rollers like a major prizefight, Rickard decided to stage the 1906 world middleweight championship between Battling Nelson and Joe Gans. Landing the fight for a $30,000 guarantee, he also took the unprecedented step of paying both men up front. The bout attracted over 8,000 fans from around the country and made $69,715. Said Rickard later: "What happened in the Gans–Nelson show made me think—how long has this been going on? From then on, whether I knew it or not, I was in the fight business." **Rickard stepped up in class** in 1910 when he promoted the most anticipated sporting event of the new century—the "Great White Hope" fight between black heavyweight champion Jack Johnson and former titleholder Jim Jeffries in Reno. Jeffries, who had been lured out of retirement by a guaranteed purse of $101,000 plus two-thirds of the movie rights (the winner would get 60 percent of the pot), was installed as the favorite but took a terrible beating before being counted out in the 15th round. A crowd of 15,760 paid a record $270,775 to watch the mismatch, but as news of Johnson's victory spread across the country there were several race riots and 19 blacks were killed. Most states refused to allow the film of the fight to be shown. **Johnson, who flaunted**

1910

JAN. 5
Montreal Canadiens play their first National Hockey Association game, beating Cobalt Silver Kings, 7–6, at Jubilee Arena in Montreal.

MAR. 16
Driving a Benz auto, Barney Oldfield sets new land speed record of 131.7 miles per hour over one-mile course at Daytona Beach, Fla.

APRIL 14
William Howard Taft becomes first American president to throw out ceremonial first pitch of season. Washington Senators pitcher Walter Johnson catches Taft's toss then throws one-hitter at visiting Chicago White Sox.

JULY 4
Former heavyweight champion and "Great White Hope" Jim Jeffries returns to ring after five-year retirement but is knocked out in 15th round of bout in Reno with black champion Jack Johnson.

OCT. 9
While unpopular Ty Cobb sits out final two games of regular season to protect his American League-leading .383 batting average, Cleveland's Nap Lajoie goes 8-for-8 in season-ending doubleheader against St. Louis to finish with an average of .384. Among Lajoie's hits are six "gift" bunt singles courtesy of a pulled-back Browns' infield. A week later, an angry A.L. president Ban Johnson awards batting title to Cobb, announcing his final average was actually .385.

OCT. 23
Philadelphia Athletics win their first World Series title as pitchers Jack Combs (3–0) and Chief Bender (1–1) combine for five complete-game outings.

1911

MAY 30
Ray Harroun, driving a six-cylinder Marmon Wasp, captures first running of Indianapolis 500-mile auto race, winning in six hours, 42 minutes, eight seconds. His average speed is 74.602 miles per hour.

JUNE 24
John McDermott becomes first American-born golfer to win U.S. Open. The 21-year-old former caddie, who lost an 18-hole playoff for title to Alex Smith in 1910, wins three-way playoff at Chicago Golf Club.

SEPT. 3
Bill Larned wins his fifth straight U.S. Tennis Championship and seventh overall a month after Hazel Hotchkiss captures her third consecutive women's singles title.

OCT. 6
Cy Young loses final game of his 22-year career as Boston Braves drop 13–3 decision to Brooklyn. Baseball's all-time winning pitcher retires with a record of 511–316.

Jeffries–Johnson promoters J. J. Gleason (left) and Tex Rickard

NOV. 11
Tiny Carlisle Indian School of Pennsylvania upsets Harvard, 18–15, in Cambridge, Mass. Halfback Jim Thorpe kicks four field goals, including game-winner from 48 yards out.

1912

APRIL 20
Fenway Park in Boston and Navin Park in Detroit open as Red Sox and Tigers win before crowds of 27,000 and 24,384, respectively.

JULY 20
Hawaiian surfing legend Duke Kahanamoku follows up his gold-medal swimming performance in 100 meters at Stockholm by setting new world record of 1:01.6 on a straight course.

OCT. 16
Smokey Joe Wood, a 34-game winner during regular season, wins three more times in World Series as Boston Red Sox beat New York Giants, four games to three with one tied. Dropping of routine fly ball by Giants' center fielder Fred Snodgrass in bottom of 10th inning of deciding game sets up Red Sox victory.

MAR. 13
Quebec Bulldogs sweep Moncton in two games to win first Stanley Cup competition featuring two teams skating six a-side and with three 20-minute periods.

JULY 15
Jim Thorpe wins decathlon gold medal a week after placing first in pentathlon at Olympic Games in Stockholm. While Games include electronic timing and public address system for first time, Swedish organizers refuse to permit boxing matches.

AUG. 26
Maurice McLaughlin and Mary K. Browne win singles titles at U.S. Tennis Championships in first tournament where defending champions are required to play through entire draw instead of just meeting winner of challenge round.

1913

JULY 28
Davis Cup returns to United States after 11-year absence as Americans defeat defending champion British Isles, 3–2, in challenge round.

JAN. 27
Jim Thorpe admits he played minor league baseball for $25 a game during summer vacations from Carlisle Indian School in 1909 and 1910. He is promptly stripped of his medals and records from 1912 Stockholm Olympics.

SEPT. 30
America's Francis Ouimet, a 20-year-old sporting goods employee and amateur golfer, defeats British professionals Harry Vardon and Ted Ray in three-way playoff to win the U.S. Open at the Country Club in Brookline, Mass.

his status and his penchant for white women, was convicted on a trumped-up morals charge in 1912 and fled to Canada. Broke and out of shape after three years on the lam, he fought Jess Willard in Havana in 1915 and lost his title—probably on purpose, either for money or the misguided hope that by losing he would see his conviction dropped. Rickard had nothing to do with the Havana bout, but reappeared in 1919 to promote Willard's second and final title defense against a 24-year-old brawler from Manassa, Colorado, named Jack Dempsey. A crowd of 45,000 showed up in Toledo to watch Dempsey destroy Willard in three rounds. ❧ **Rickard's promotions proved** there was money to be made in spectator sports and that professional fun and games had now become a durable part of the landscape. The Kentucky Derby regularly drew over 40,000 racing fans and their wallets to Louisville. In 1911, a crowd of 80,000 witnessed the first Indianapolis 500 at an all-brick, 2½-mile test track in the nation's leading automotive city. Five years later, the new Professional Golfers Association held its first pros-only PGA Championship in Bronxville, New York. And in Canada, the trustees of the Stanley Cup decided in 1914 that only professional leagues could compete for hockey's biggest prize. ❧ **In baseball, major league owners** were so confident in the future that 13 of the 16 American and National League teams moved into

Ty Cobb, fierce even at rest

Once there was a ballpark in Brooklyn.

new concrete-and-steel ballparks between 1909 and 1915. Unfortunately, expenditures for the safety and comfort of the game's expanding fan base didn't trickle down to the performers. Player complaints about low pay, no pensions, and a reserve clause that bound them to their teams indefinitely fell largely on deaf ears, and no owner was harder of hearing than Charles A. Comiskey of the Chicago White Sox. As a result, a decade that opened in style with President Taft throwing out the first ball of the 1910 season ended in disgrace with the White Sox throwing the 1919 World Series. ✎ Gambling fueled the early century sports boom as sure as gasoline powered Barney Oldfield's Blitzen Benz to a world record of over 131 miles per hour at Daytona Beach in 1910. All sports, from cards and craps to boxing and billiards, were considered games of chance and worth a wager, especially if you had an edge. Sportsmen bet and the biggest bettors were regarded as the biggest sportsmen—plungers like "Bet a Million" Gates, "Titanic" Thompson, and Arnold Rothstein. Most events were on the up-and-up, but some were not. Baseball was no different. Players associated openly with gamblers and a few were known to take money for services rendered. Given that atmosphere, dumping a World Series was just raising the stakes. Only this time, the conspirators got caught. ✎ Since the Black Sox scandal wasn't uncovered until 1920, the decade's most newsworthy transgression centered around one of the century's greatest athletes, Jim Thorpe. A Sac

NOV. 1
Notre Dame stuns college football with its unprecedented passing attack as quarterback Gus Dorais completes 14 of 17 attempts for 243 yards to defeat Army 35–13 at West Point. One of his completions is a 35-yard touchdown strike to end and Irish captain Knute Rockne.

1914

APRIL 13
Federal League opens inaugural season as baseball's third major league with eight new teams playing in eight new ballparks. Well-heeled owners raid several N.L. and A.L. rosters for players.

JULY 4
Harvard's eight-man crew becomes first American boat to win Grand Challenge Cup at Henley Royal Regatta in England.

AUG. 21
Walter Hagan captures first major golf tournament of his career, beating Chick Evans by a stroke in U.S. Open.

AUG. 15
Maurice McLoughlin beats Norman Brookes of Australia and Tony Wilding of New Zealand in singles, but Australasia defeats the U.S., 3–2, to win Davis Cup challenge round for fifth time.

OCT. 13
Boston's "Miracle Braves," who were in National League cellar on July 18, complete worst-to-first turnaround by sweeping Philadelphia A's out of World Series.

1915

FEBRUARY
Skating's first major ice show, "Flirting in St. Moritz," opens at Hippodrome in New York and runs for 300 days.

MAR. 26
Vancouver Millionaires of Pacific Coast Hockey Association complete three-game sweep of National Hockey Association's Ottawa Senators to win Stanley Cup.

APRIL 5
Challenger Jess Willard knocks out 37-year-old heavyweight champion Jack Johnson in 26th round of their bout in Havana, Cuba.

JULY
Wimbledon tennis and British Open golf tournaments are among many sporting events cancelled for duration of World War I.

SEPT. 8
Men's singles competition in U.S. Tennis Championships moved from Newport to Forest Hills, N.Y. Bill Johnston defeats Maurice McLoughlin for title at West Side Tennis Club.

OCT. 3
Ty Cobb steals his 96th base of season to establish record that will stand until 1962. He also sets record for times caught stealing with 38.

DEC. 22
Federal League reaches agreement with American and National Leagues to cease operation after two seasons. In return, AL and NL owners agree to buy back players who jumped to FL, and allow Chicago Whales owner Charles Weeghman to buy NL Cubs and St. Louis Terriers owner Phil Ball to buy AL Browns.

1916

MAR. 30
Montreal Canadiens win their first Stanley Cup title, beating Portland Rosebuds of PCHA, three games to two.

JAN. 1
After an absence of 14 years, Rose Bowl game is renewed and Washington State shuts out Brown University and its great black All-America halfback Fritz Pollard, 14–0.

OCT. 7
In most lopsided college football game of century, Georgia Tech beats tiny Cumberland College of Lebanon, Tenn., 222–0. Cumberland made trip to Atlanta with only 15 players.

SEPT. 9
Chick Evans wins U.S. Amateur Championship in Merion Cricket Club outside Philadelphia, becoming first player to claim U.S. Open and Amateur tennis titles in same calendar year.

OCT. 12
Boston Red Sox win second straight World Series, beating Brooklyn Robins in five games.

OCT. 14
Englishman Jim Barnes defeats Scotsman Jock Hutchison, 1–up, to win inaugural PGA Championship for touring golf professionals.

NOV. 4
Visiting Illinois shocks unbeaten Minnesota, 14–9. The Gophers entered contest averaging 50 points a game.

1917

MAR. 25
Seattle Metropolitans of PCHA become first U.S.-based team to win Stanley Cup, beating Montreal Canadiens, three games to one.

MAY 2
A gathering of 3,500 fans at Chicago's Weeghman Park witnesses baseball's first double no-hitter as Cincinnati's Fred Toney and the Cubs' Hippo Vaughn both toss gems. In top of 10th inning Reds score on a single, two errors, and a swinging bunt. Toney retires all three Cubs in bottom half for 1–0, no-hit victory.

MAY 28
Benny Leonard knocks out Freddie Welch in 9th round to win world lightweight championship, a title he will hold until 1925.

John Heisman, coach for 36 years; his 1916 Georgia Tech team won a game 222–0.

and Fox Indian from the Oklahoma Territory, Thorpe first gained national attention in 1911 as an All-America halfback at Carlisle Indian School in Pennsylvania. A year later, he went to Stockholm as a member of the United States Olympic team and easily won gold medals in the decathlon and pentathlon. When the king of Sweden said he was "the greatest athlete in the world" and President Taft called him "the highest type of citizen," nobody argued. That fall, Thorpe led Carlisle to a 12–1–1 record that included a 27–6 thrashing of Army at West Point. ✽

Jim Thorpe

Then early in 1913,

a newspaper revealed that Thorpe had played semipro baseball for $25 a game in 1909 and 1910. Left unsaid was that he had been too naïve to play under an assumed name as many college players did to avoid detection. The Amateur Athletic Union branded Thorpe a professional and supported the International Olympic Committee's demand that he return their medals. Now the world's most notorious professional, Thorpe played six years of major league baseball and, from 1915 to 1928, top-flight professional football, including in the nascent National Football League. ✽ **Pro and amateur golfers played** together as usual in the 1913 United States Open at the Country Club in Brookline, Massachusetts, but for the first time an amateur won. Francis Ouimet, a local 20-year-old sporting goods store employee who grew up caddying at the club but wasn't a member, tied seasoned British pros Harry Varden and Ted Ray after 72 holes, then won an 18-hole playoff by five strokes.

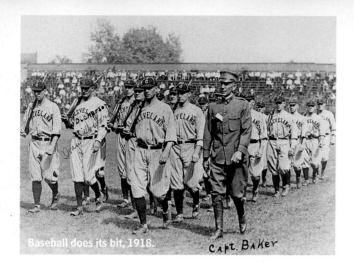
Baseball does its bit, 1918.

Capt. Baker

The unexpected victory, by a blue-collar kid whose 10-year-old caddie had to skip school to work the extra round, was the turning point of the century in American golf. It not only signaled the end of British rule in the sport, but it also wrested the game from the clutches of the privileged and gave it to the public.

✒ The year after Ouimet's win,

World War I erupted in Europe and lasted through 1918. The United States didn't send troops until mid-1917, and while many American athletes volunteered for military duty, some famous figures like Dempsey and Boston Red Sox pitcher Babe Ruth were called slackers when they did not. One of those who did enlist was racecar driver Eddie Rickenbacker, who had participated in five of the first six Indianapolis 500s. Starting out as Colonel General Billy Mitchell's chauffeur, Rickenbacker talked Mitchell into sending him to flight school, then assigning him to the famous 94th Aero Pursuit "Hat in the Ring" Squadron. Shooting down 22 German planes in less than seven months, he returned from Europe as America's "Ace of Aces." ✒

Upset and Man o' War

JUNE 23
Ernie Shore of Boston Red Sox pitches perfect game against Washington in relief of starter Babe Ruth. Ruth walked lead-off man Eddie Foster and was ejected from game after punching plate umpire Brick Owens in an argument over fourth ball. Shore came on, Foster was thrown out trying to steal second and the next 26 Senators' batters are retired in order.

JUNE 22
Molla Bjurstedt becomes first woman to win four consecutive singles titles at U.S. Tennis Championships.

SEPT. 11
Boston Red Sox win third World Series championship in four years and fourth title of decade, downing Chicago Cubs in six games. Boston pitcher Babe Ruth sets Series record of 29 $\frac{2}{3}$ scoreless innings.

1918

OCT. 15
New York Giants lose their fourth World Series of decade in six games to Chicago White Sox.

NOV. 26
Five-team National Hockey League is organized in Montreal hotel room and will begin play on Dec. 19. Quebec opts not to field team for two years, and Montreal Wanderers will withdraw six games into 1917–18 season when Montreal Arena burns down.

AUG. 24
Secretary of War Newton D. Baker announces that baseball will be allowed to play World Series, but 10 percent of all profits must go to war charities. Earlier, Baker ruled baseball was not an essential industry and ordered major leagues to end regular season by September 1.

NOV. 11
Armistice signed ending World War I.

1919

JUNE 11
Sir Barton wins Belmont Stakes by five lengths to become first three-year-old to win Kentucky Derby, Preakness, and Belmont. Jockey Johnny Loftus is aboard for all three races.

AUG. 12
Man o' War suffers lone defeat of his two-year, 21-race career when Upset beats him in Sanford Memorial Stakes at Saratoga.

APR. 1
Deciding game of Stanley Cup finals is cancelled due to influenza epidemic that claims 548,000 lives in U.S. and 20 million worldwide. Montreal Canadiens of NHL and Seattle Millionaires of PCHA were tied at two wins apiece and a draw.

JULY 4
Jack Dempsey, 13 years younger and 58 pounds lighter than heavyweight champion Jess Willard, knocks Willard down seven times in first round and goes on to win title with a TKO in the 4th round.

OCT. 9
Underdog Cincinnati Reds beat Chicago White Sox, five games to three, in best-of-nine World Series. Eight "Black Sox" players will later be thrown out of baseball for conspiring with gamblers to throw the Series.

Babe Ruth, Red Sox pitcher

Shown here with caddy Eddie Lowery at the Brookline Country Club in 1913, 20-year-old Francis Ouimet (right) had been a caddy at Brookline himself just a few years before. A complete unknown, the American novice tied British pros Harry Vardon and Ted Ray, then went on to defeat them in an 18-hole playoff.

As the decade wore on, the fancy set gravitated to field sports, especially golf and tennis. But the working man's sanctuary remained the smoky pool hall; the obligatory sign warning boys to keep out serves as testament to its allure.

A pool table may have spelled trouble for American youth, but Jake Schaefer, Jr., grew up with a cue in his hand. His father had been one of the best balkline players of the previous century; Young Jake went on to win 13 titles of his own and join his dad in the Hall of Fame.

Jim Thorpe is captured in flight at the Stockholm Games of 1912, piling up points in the long jump. He won the pentathlon and the decathlon with such ease that King Gustaf V was prompted to say, "You, sir, are the greatest athlete in the world." Thorpe's reply: "Thanks, King." Because it was later revealed that he had accepted pocket money to play minor league baseball, Thorpe's medals were revoked.

In 1904 the 15-year-old Jim Thorpe left Oklahoma for the Carlisle Indian Industrial School in Pennsylvania. There, under the tutelage of Glenn "Pop" Warner (top left, next to Thorpe), he and his vocational-school mates became a college football powerhouse.

The great one in action. Thorpe scored 25 touchdowns for national champion Carlisle in 1912, then went on to the New York Giants baseball team in 1913. Two years later he joined the Canton Bulldogs to begin a fabled pro football career.

Fatally stricken after his final game for Notre Dame, in 1920, George Gipp told Rockne, "when the breaks are beating the boys, tell them to win one for the Gipper." Eight years later, trailing Army at the half, Rockne told the story to his team, which rallied to win. Or so the story goes.

Knute Rockne was the dominant football coach of his era. From 1918 until his death in an airplane crash in 1931, his Fighting Irish won 105 games while losing only 12. Rockne's fiery, inspirational style, often emulated, has never been duplicated.

Wilbur "Fats" Henry was a giant of his day in every respect. Weighing in at 250 pounds, he was an All-America tackle and dropkicker for Washington & Jefferson in 1918–19.

Harlem Tommy Murphy (137 pounds, left) and Abe Attell (118 pounds) battled to a 20-round draw in San Francisco on August 3, 1912. Attell had been featherweight champ for a decade; today he is more famed as one of the fixers, with Arnold Rothstein, of the 1919 World Series.

Wrestling from 1904 to 1947, Ed "Strangler" Lewis was a five-time champion who appeared in more than 6,200 matches and lost only 33. His trademark headlock, he once said, was "a knockout just as soporific as a solid punch to the jaw."

Charles Conlon's classic photo of Ty Cobb sliding into third has been recorded in the annals as taking place in 1910 at Highlanders Park in New York. Jimmy Austin, the third baseman in the play, recalled 50 years later, "Look at Cobb's face. That guy wanted to win in the worst way."

Buck Weaver of the Chicago White Sox tries to avert a tag in Game 2 of the 1919 World Series. Seven Chicago players agreed to accept bribes to play less than their best. Weaver always maintained that he had played to win, but because he had had prior knowledge of the fix, he ended up one of the Black Sox, banned from baseball for life.

Addie Joss, 31, was one of the best pitchers in the game when he was stricken by meningitis and died at the beginning of the 1911 season. Later that summer, American Leaguers formed an All-Star team to play in Cleveland to raise money for Joss' family.

Baseball was booming in the first half of the decade. Peace between the American and National leagues had fostered prosperity, workers had leisure time and spare change, and magnates, seeing standing-room only crowds, were moved to build new stadiums everywhere.

Maurice "Red" McLoughlin of the U.S. was the first to play the "modern" game of tennis on grass—serve, rush the net, volley, and go for passing shots. Here he contends in the U.S. Open at Forest Hills against Richard Williams (right). Yet even as sport was becoming a modern, urban institution with increasing interest for spectators, the rural field-day tussles of the previous century were still in evidence, such as this tug o' war in Brooklyn.

In the 1890s many "Bloomer Girls" baseball teams cropped up all over the country, and the loose-fitting, Turkish style costumes were modest and practical for gymnastics and basketball, too. In the 1910s, however, the "female base ballists" exchanged their flowing garb for baseball gear. Bloomer Girls teams barnstormed the country, often with male players "passing" as Bloomerites, till the mid-1930s.

As voices grew louder for women's suffrage at decade's end, distaff athletes were unafraid to invade even that bastion of manhood, the bowling saloon or alley, and to compete for their own championship. Cuspidors were probably moved out of sight for the occasion.

Archery was viewed as a refined, sedate sport, providing fresh air and healthful exercise, and thus suitable for young women, much as croquet, lawn bowls, and quoits. In 1916 women took up trapshooting, and the vote seemed not very far off at all.

1920–1929

Power incarnate: the mighty Hack Wilson

1920–1929

1920

In January of 1920 Babe Ruth was traded to the Yankees and Prohibition became the law of the land. Both acts, the Volstead and the Bambino's, ushered in an era of bootleg liquor and sporting heroics that intoxicated the nation. **If America accepted sin** in the twenties, then Ruth was its favorite sinner. He spent more time at speakeasies and whorehouses than he did at the ballpark, but he misbehaved with a nudge and a wink, and as long as he hit home runs the public loved him. After a brutal war in Europe and a worldwide flu epidemic that had claimed half a million American lives, the country was behind the Babe when it came to having a good time. **The work week was down** to 48 hours, and the stock market was rising faster than one of Robert Goddard's new rockets. Women, who had come into the labor force during the wartime manpower shortage, were now drinking and smoking in public and voting for president just like the men. Credit was easy and jazz was hard to resist. Movies could talk and radio was in its infancy. Automobile production was up, but so was the rate of lawlessness. Prohibition was boom time for a lot of industries, including organized crime. **But no industry captured the public's daily attention** as sports did, and the twenties were proclaimed "The Golden Age of Sport." Years later, in a book called *The Golden People*, one of the era's best-known sportswriters, Paul Gallico, wrote: "This remarkable ten years saw the most fabulous set of champions arise in every game, amateur or professional, not only from the point of view of performance, but of character as well. Every one was a colorful extrovert of one kind or another. Each had a romance connected with him or her, and these legends themselves were reflections of our age of innocence, for they were all success stories,

FEB. 13
The Negro National League (chartered as National Association of Colored Professional Baseball Clubs) is organized during meeting at YMCA in Kansas City, Mo.

JAN. 3
New York Yankees purchase contract of 26-year-old pitcher-outfielder Babe Ruth from Boston Red Sox for $125,000.

AUG. 16
Cleveland shortstop Ray Chapman, 29, is struck in head by Carl Mays fastball in game with Yankees at Polo Grounds in New York. Chapman never regains consciousness and dies next day from a fractured skull.

MAY 24
The Walker Law, a bill legalizing boxing and regulating its conduct in New York State, is signed by Governor Al Smith.

SEPT. 12
First Olympics since World War I conclude in Antwerp, Belgium. United States wins 95 medals, including 41 golds.

SEPT. 17
The American Professional Football Association, forerunner of the NFL, is founded in Ralph Hay's Hupmobile showroom in Canton, Ohio. Twelve teams pay $100 each to secure franchises.

SEPT. 28
In what will come to be known as the Black Sox Scandal, eight Chicago White Sox players are indicted on charges of conspiring to fix the 1919 World Series.

OCT. 1
New York Yankees become first baseball team to draw one million customers, ending season with attendance of 1,289,422 at Polo Grounds.

OCT. 10
Cleveland second baseman Bill Wambsganss completes only unassisted triple play in World Series history.

OCT. 21
Man o' War defeats 1919 Triple Crown winner Sir Barton by seven lengths in match race over one and a quarter miles at Kenilworth Race Track in Windsor, Ontario. Man o' War wins a purse of $75,000 and is retired following the race.

NOV. 12
Major league baseball owners hire federal judge Kenesaw Mountain Landis as first commissioner.

DEC. 13
Challenger Ed (Strangler) Lewis pins heavyweight wrestling champion Joe Stecher in two-hour, catch-as-catch-can match at Madison Square Garden.

1921

JULY 2
Heavyweight champion Jack Dempsey knocks out Frenchman Georges Carpentier in 4th round before over 90,000 at Boyle's Thirty Acres in Jersey City, N.J. The bout attracts boxing's first million-dollar gate and is carried on radio.

AUG. 2
Chicago jury acquits eight Black Sox defendants of throwing 1919 World Series. After hearing verdict, however, Commissioner Kenesaw Mountain Landis bans all eight from baseball for life.

AUG. 5
With announcer Harold Arlin at the microphone, baseball's first major league game is broadcast from Pittsburgh's Forbes Field on radio station KDKA. Pirates beat Philadelphia Phillies, 8–5.

SEPT. 28
Walter Hagen becomes first American-born professional golfer to win PGA Championship.

OCT. 29
The Praying Colonels of little Centre College in Danville, Ky., upset unbeaten Harvard, 6–0, on a third-quarter touchdown.

OCT. 13
New York Giants win first one-city World Series since 1906, five games to three, over Yankees at Polo Grounds. Series is also first broadcast on radio with Grantland Rice and Graham McNamee announcing.

1922

APR. 16
Sharpshooter Annie Oakley, who starred in Buffalo Bill Cody's Wild West Show from 1885 to 1902, establishes unofficial women's world record by breaking 100 clay targets in a row at trapshooting demonstration in Pinehurst, N.C.

JUNE 23
Seventeen-year-old swimmer Johnny Weissmuller of Illinois Athletic Club breaks four world records in Honolulu meet at distances of 300 and 400 meters and 440 and 500 yards.

JUNE 23
Walter Hagen becomes first American-born golfer to win British Open, besting field at Royal St. George's in Sandwich, England.

JUNE 24
The American Professional Football Association officially changes name to National Football League and Chicago Staleys' co-owner George Halas renames club the Bears.

AUG. 28
Walker Cup matches between amateur golfers of U.S. and Great Britain are played for first time. Americans win at National Golf Links in Southampton, N.Y.

AUG. 18
Twenty-year-old Gene Sarazen defeats Emmet French to win PGA Championship a month after beating 20-year-old amateur Bobby Jones to capture the U.S. Open. Sarazen is first golfer to win both the Open and PGA title in same year.

OCT. 28
Princeton, making its first intersectional trip to the Midwest, rallies for two touchdowns in fourth quarter to defeat unbeaten Chicago, 21–18.

Bigger than baseball, the Babe became the nation's hero.

Walter Hagen waits his turn.

the great American fairy tale, the rise from rags to riches, the first such actually dramatized before our eyes." ❧ **Those champions included** Ruth in baseball; Jack Dempsey and Gene Tunney in boxing; Knute Rockne and Red Grange in football; Suzanne Lenglen, Helen Wills, and Bill Tilden in tennis; Bobby Jones and Walter Hagen in golf; Johnny Weissmuller and Gertrude Ederle in swimming; Tommy Hitchcock in polo; Alf Goullet in six-day bicycle racing; and Man o' War, the superhorse of the first half-century, whose only loss in 21 races over a two-year career made the horse that beat him—Upset—synonymous with defeating the favorite. ❧ **The top international performer** of the decade was distance runner Paavo Nurmi of Finland, who set 22 official and 13 unofficial world records in distances from 1,500 meters to 20 kilometers, and won nine gold medals in three Olympics. Famous for his severe training regimen and running with a stopwatch in his hand, "the Flying Finn" barnstormed the U.S. in the winter of 1925, winning 53 of 55 races and setting 12 world indoor bests in three months over all distances from 1,500 to 5,000 meters. ❧ **His Olympic career ended** when he was barred from the 1932 Olympics in Los Angeles after receiving excessive expense money on a 1929 trip to Germany. The ruling by the International Olympic Committee came as no surprise to the track world, where it was often said that Nurmi "had the lowest heartbeat and the highest asking price" of any athlete in the world. ❧ **Before Ruth got to New York,** no baseball player had ever hit as many as 30 home runs in a single season. In the twenties he averaged 46 homers a year, including his high-water mark of 60 in 1927. The Yankees, who had never won a pennant before, went to the World Series six times and won three championships. They also built 62,000-seat Yankee Stadium to hold the huge crowds that wanted to see the Sultan of Swat do just that. ❧

Ruth's home runs helped save baseball,
along with the appointment of flinty federal judge Kenesaw Mountain Landis as commissioner. The conspiracy to fix the 1919 World Series was uncovered by a Chicago grand jury in 1920 and badly shook the public's confidence in the major leagues. "Baseball is something more than a game to an American boy," said Landis after taking office. "It is his training field for life work.

Judge Landis

Destroy his faith in its squareness and honesty and you have destroyed something more; you have planted suspicion of all things in his heart." ❧

The eight Chicago White Sox players
who either participated in throwing the

The Black Sox and their lawyers

Series or knew about the fix and said nothing were put on trial in 1921 for defrauding the public (there were no laws against dumping ball games) and acquitted. The night the Black Sox

1923

JAN. 10
American Amateur Union (AAU) begins to register women athletes in all sports under its jurisdiction.

APR. 18
Yankee Stadium opens in Bronx with 74,200 on hand (a reported 25,000 others are turned away). Babe Ruth christens new ballpark with a three-run homer in a 4–1 victory over Boston.

JULY 15
Amateur Bobby Jones wins his first major golf championship, defeating Bobby Cruickshank, 76–78, in 18-hole playoff for U.S. Open.

SEPT. 14
In one of the fiercest heavyweight championship fights ever, Jack Dempsey knocks out challenger Luis Firpo at 0:57 of second round before 85,000 at Polo Grounds. Dempsey sent Firpo to the canvas seven times in first round before Firpo rose up and stunned the champion by knocking him through the ropes and into press row.

1924

MAR. 25
Montreal Canadiens complete sweep of western powers Vancouver and Calgary to win first Stanley Cup since 1916. Rookie sensation Howie Morenz scores seven goals in six postseason games.

JAN. 26
American speed skater Charles Jewtraw wins first gold medal of new Winter Olympic Games at Chamonix, France, with victory in 500-meter sprint. Norway and Finland claim 27 of 43 medals awarded at the 11-day competition.

JULY 27
Distance runner Paavo Nurmi of Finland wins five gold medals as star performer of Summer Olympics in Paris.

SEPT. 30
St. Louis Cardinals shortstop Rogers Hornsby finishes the regular season with .424 batting average, the highest of century.

OCT. 10
Washington Senators win their only World Series ever, beating New York Giants in Game 7 by a 4–3 score in 12 innings. Walter Johnson pitches four shutout innings in relief to get victory.

OCT. 18
Sportswriter Grantland Rice dubs Notre Dame backfield of Stuhldreher, Miller, Crowley, and Layden, "The Four Horsemen," after unbeaten Fighting Irish defeat Army, 13–7. That same afternoon Illinois halfback Red Grange runs for 262 yards and four touchdowns the first four times he touches the ball as the Illini rout Michigan, 39–14.

DEC. 1
The National Hockey League opens its seventh season with its first U.S. franchise, the Boston Bruins, defeating the Montreal Maroons, 2–1, at Boston Arena.

1925

MAY 30
Driver Peter DePaolo becomes first winner of Indianapolis 500 to average over 100 miles per hour for entire race. Official average speed of his Duesenberg Special is 101.13 mph.

SEPT. 19
Bill Tilden wins U.S. Tennis Championships at Forest Hills for sixth consecutive year, defeating Davis Cup teammate Bill Johnston in final for fourth straight title.

NOV. 15
Pro basketball's first major league, the nine-team American Basketball League, opens its inaugural season.

NOV. 22
Illinois halfback Red Grange, college football's premier player, signs pro football contract with Chicago Bears the day after his final collegiate game. Deal guarantees Grange $100,000 for remaining two games of NFL season and a 17-game barnstorming tour in December and January.

DEC. 15
The third Madison Square Garden, this one on Eighth Avenue between 49th and 50th streets, officially opens as a crowd of 17,442 sees NHL game between New York Americans and Montreal Canadiens. Montreal wins, 3–1.

1926

MAR. 7
In a match pairing the best professional and best amateur in golf, Walter Hagen defeats Bobby Jones, 12-up with 11 holes to play in a two-day, 72-hole exhibition on two Florida golf courses.

FEB. 26
Six-time Wimbledon women's champion Suzanne Lenglen defeats three-time U.S. champion Helen Wills, 6–3, 8–6, in an exhibition match at Cannes, France. Lenglen, 26, will turn pro in fall and tour America, while Wills, 20, will win eight Wimbledon singles titles between 1927 and 1938.

MAY 12
At age 38, Walter Johnson becomes only second pitcher to win 400 games, beating the St. Louis Browns, 7–4. Only Cy Young won more major league games.

JULY 10
Bobby Jones captures U.S. Open by a stroke over John Turnesa to become first golfer to win U.S. and British Opens in same year.

Howie Morenz of the Montreal Canadiens, hockey's Babe Ruth

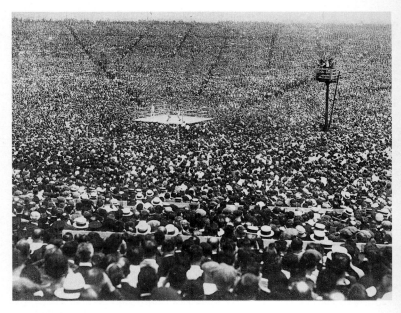

Dempsey vs. Carpentier, 1921

got off, Landis banished them all from baseball for life. ❧ **Besides baseball,** the two big mass-spectator sports were boxing and college football. In the twenties, Jack Dempsey fought four heavyweight title fights that together drew well over 400,000 fans, while colleges with major football programs went on a building spree that erected mammoth stadiums from coast to coast, most of which still stand. ❧ **With master promoter Tex Rickard** beating the publicity drums for each fight, Dempsey knocked out French war hero Georges Carpentier in 1921 and Argentina's Luis Firpo in 1923. After a three-year layoff he then lost two 10-round decisions to Gene Tunney, the first witnessed in the rain by 115,000 in Philadelphia and the second a year later before 150,000 in Chicago. The Carpentier fight was boxing's first million-dollar gate. The second Tunney fight, the "Battle of the Long Count," was boxing's first two-million-dollar gate and was heard by a radio audience of 50 million. ❧ **Dempsey retired** after the second defeat and Rickard returned to New York, where he had been running Madison Square Garden since 1920 and had just opened a new 17,000-seat arena by the same name in 1925. Boxing shows paid the bills, but the Garden also featured pro wrestling (still a legitimate sport back then) six-day bicycle races, track meets, rodeos, dog shows, political conventions, and, beginning in 1925, the National Hockey League. ❧ **In football, the darling of the decade** was All-America halfback Red Grange of Illinois. Like Dempsey, Grange filled stadiums wherever he went. He established himself as the game's best player in 1924 when he single-handedly destroyed Michigan, 39–14, with touchdown runs of 95, 67, 56, 45, and 15 yards. ❧ **The next year,** Grange stunned his admirers by signing a professional contract with the Chicago Bears of the six-year-old National Football League that guaranteed him $100,000 of the gate receipts for the remainder of the Bears' regular season and a series of exhibition games afterward. The deal set off a storm of protest by pious college officials who felt football should not be played for pay, but Grange and personal manager C.C. ("Cash and Carry") Pyle saw the opportunity to get rich quick and took it. In return the NFL got attention, especially in New York and Los Angeles, where crowds of over 70,000 came out to see the Galloping Ghost in the flesh. ❧ **Subsequent moves by Pyle** and his client were not so successful. Unable to get a piece of the Bears or an NFL expansion franchise in New York, they leased Yankee Stadium in 1926 and built a rival league of nine teams around Grange. The American Football League folded after one season and Grange returned to the NFL. ❧ **Pyle, however,** continued to look for another big score. In 1926, he signed six-time Wimbledon champion Suzanne Lenglen for $75,000 and organized the first pro tennis tour around her. He also tried to lure Bill Tilden, the top men's player in the world, from the amateur ranks, but Tilden's asking price was too high. The Lenglen tour lasted only a few

AUG. 6
American Gertrude Ederle becomes first woman to swim English Channel. Her time of 14 hours and 39 minutes breaks previous record by over two hours.

SEPT. 16
France's Henri Cochet ends Bill Tilden's six-year reign as U.S. singles champion in quarterfinals. The defeat comes five days after Tilden led U.S. to its seventh straight Davis Cup championship, beating Cochet and France in Philadelphia.

SEPT. 23
Jack Dempsey, defending his heavyweight championship for first time in three years, loses a unanimous 10-round decision to Gene Tunney before rain-soaked crowd of 120,000 in Philadelphia.

OCT. 10
Aging St. Louis pitcher Grover Cleveland Alexander, 39, comes on in relief in seventh inning of World Series Game 7 to preserve a 3–2 Cardinal victory over the New York Yankees. He strikes out Tony Lazzeri with the bases loaded and two outs and then holds Yanks scoreless rest of the way.

1927

JUNE 4
Led by Gene Sarazen and playing captain Walter Hagen, the United States defeats Great Britain, 9$\frac{1}{2}$ to 2$\frac{1}{2}$, in first formal Ryder Cup matches at Worcester (Mass.) Country Club.

JAN. 7
With English-born, 23-year-old Abe Saperstein serving as coach and general manager, all-black Harlem Globetrotters play their first official pro basketball game in Hinckley, Ill.

JULY 18
Playing for Philadelphia A's, 40-year-old Ty Cobb doubles off Sam Gibson of Detroit for 4,000th hit of his career.

SEPT. 22
Gene Tunney retains heavyweight title by unanimous 10-round decision in rematch with Jack Dempsey at Soldier Field in Chicago. A crowd of 150,000 sees ex-Marine benefit from controversial "Long Count" in seventh round when Dempsey knocks him down but refuses to go immediately to neutral corner.

SEPT. 30
Babe Ruth hits record 60th home run of season off Washington pitcher Tom Zachary in New York. Yankees win American League pennant with 110–44 record and go on to sweep World Series against Pittsburgh.

NOV. 5
Walter Hagen wins fifth PGA Championship and fourth in a row. No other golfer during the century won a major championship in four consecutive years.

1928

FEB. 18
Sonja Henie of Norway wins her first figure skating gold medal and Sweden's Gilles Grafstrom wins his third in a row (including 1920 Summer Games) at Winter Olympics in St. Moritz.

JULY 26
Heavyweight champion Gene Tunney knocks out Tom Heeney in 11th round at Polo Grounds in New York. The 31-year-old Tunney will retire later in the year.

OCT. 3
Leo Diegel ends Walter Hagen's 22-match unbeaten streak in quarterfinals of PGA Championship, then beats Gene Sarazen and Al Espinoza to win his first major title.

APRIL 14
New York Rangers win their first Stanley Cup, beating Montreal Maroons in five games. In Game 2, New York's 2–1 overtime win featured 44-year-old coach Lester Patrick replacing injured goalie Lorne Chabot early in second period and stopping 18 of 19 shots in 46 minutes.

AUG. 12
Germany is allowed to return to the Olympics and women are permitted to compete in track and field events for the first time at Summer Games in Amsterdam.

1929

MAY 27
Great Britain defeats United States, 7–5, in second Ryder Cup match in Leeds, England.

AUG. 24
Helen Wills beats Phoebe Watson to win her sixth U.S. Championship and sweep the national singles titles of France, England (Wimbledon), and America for the second year in a row.

NOV. 28
Chicago Cardinals halfback Ernie Nevers scores six touchdowns and kicks four extra points for an NFL-record 40 points as the Cards rout the cross-town Bears, 40–6, on Thanksgiving Day.

JAN. 2
In the Rose Bowl, confused California defensive lineman Roy Riegels picks up a Georgia Tech fumble and runs 64 yards in wrong direction—to the Cal 1-yard line—where he is stopped by teammate Benny Lom. Tech earns a safety on a subsequent blocked punt and wins game, 8–7, to finish the 1928 season undefeated.

OCT. 26
With 80,000 looking on at Yale Bowl, 5-foot-6, 144-pound sophomore quarterback Albie Booth rallies home team past unbeaten Army, scoring all the Elis' points in a 21–13 victory.

Glenna Collett Vare, four-time U.S. Women's Amateur champion

months, but Pyle made $80,000. Two years later, he tried to cash in on America's mania for marathons by offering $25,000 to the winner of a transcontinental foot race from Los Angeles to New York. Immediately dubbed the Bunion Derby by a skeptical press, Pyle ended up losing his shirt when only 55 entrants made it across the country and their triumphant finish at Madison Square Garden was greeted by a near-empty house. ❧ In a decade famous for hucksters, hype, and hokum, the Bunion Derby failed because Pyle either forgot or ignored the fact that what set sports apart from everyday life was its potential for the spectacular. Ruth hit prodigious home runs, Dempsey fought with breath-taking fury, and Grange left tacklers in his wake. Americans wanted authentic heroes attempting to accomplish great things . . . like 19-year-old New Yorker Gertrude Ederle trying to become the first woman to swim the English Channel, in 1926. ❧ At the time, only five men since 1875 had negotiated the 21-mile stretch of sea between Calais and Dover. Ederle had come up six miles short in her first attempt in 1925 and many observers thought she would fail again. Said *The Daily News* of London: "Even the most uncompromising champion of the rights and capacities of women must admit that in contests of physical skill, speed, and endurance, they must remain forever the weaker sex." ❧ On August 6, 1926, Trudy Ederle not only swam the Channel but broke the previous record by nearly two hours. The news of her feat made newspaper front pages all over the world and when she returned home to New York City an estimated two million people turned out for a tickertape parade in her honor. ❧ The next person to get that kind of homecoming was Charles Lindbergh. ❧

The Washington Senators had never won a pennant, so it was not surprising that their 1924 World Series tickets were closely guarded.

Lou Gehrig replaced a head-achy Wally Pipp at first base one day in 1925; the rest is legend.

John Kieran poetized in 1927: "With vim and verve he has walloped the curve from Texas to Duluth,/ Which is no small task, and I beg to ask: Was there ever a guy like Ruth?" The answer, at century's end: No.

The Chicago Cubs, absorbing a pounding at the hands of the Philadelphia A's in the 1929 World Series.

The Galloping Ghost: on October 18, 1924, Illinois halfback Red Grange carried the ball eight times for 228 yards against Michigan and scored four touchdowns, all in the first 12 minutes of the game.

California center Roy Riegels is off to the races, running 66 yards in the wrong direction with a fumble in the 1929 Rose Bowl against Georgia Tech.

The senior backfield that led Notre Dame to the national championship in 1924 (left to right): Don Miller, Elmer Layden, Jim Crowley, and Harry Stuhldreher. In a hyperbolic flight of fancy, Grantland Rice called them "The Four Horsemen."

Man o' War beating 1919 Triple Crown winner Sir Barton by seven lengths in their October 12, 1920, match race at Windsor, Ontario. Organizers got around Canada's ban on match races by calling the event the $75,000 Kenilworth Park Gold Cup and arranging for the third horse in the race, Wickford, to scratch.

The steeplechase race at Amsterdam in 1928 marked the last Olympic appearance of Finland's Paavo Nurmi, who came in second behind teammate Toivo Loukola after sharing this water hazard with Lucien Duchesne of France and Bill Spencer of the U.S.

The decade's most celebrated swimmers were America's Gertrude Ederle (above), who in 1926 became the first woman to swim the English Channel, and Johnny Weissmuller (right), who set 24 world records and won five Olympic gold medals.

One of the highest-paid athletes in the U.S. in the early twenties was Australian cyclist Alf Goullet, who commanded appearance money of up to $1,000 per day. A star performer on the six-day bicycle race circuit, Goullet won eight annual races at Madison Square Garden with six different partners from 1913 to 1923.

The country's interest in tennis and in airplane wing-walking during the Roaring Twenties found its logical extension in this 1925 aviation stunt performed 3,000 feet above Los Angeles.

Frank Lockhart, winner of the 1926 Indianapolis 500 at age 23, sits in his Stutz Blackhawk Special before attempting to break the world land speed record at Daytona Beach.

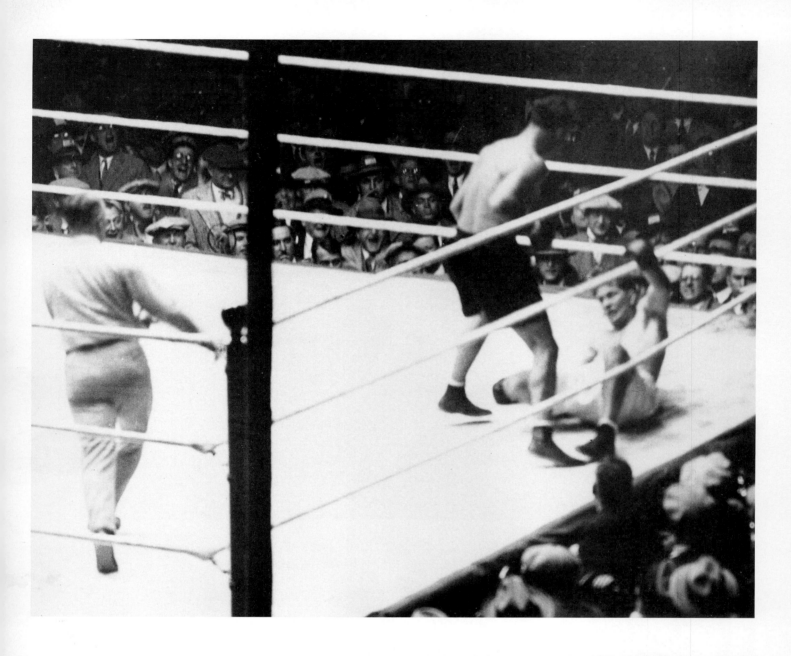

The most controversial 14 seconds of the decade, if not the century, took place in the 1927 heavyweight rematch between Jack Dempsey and champion Gene Tunney at Chicago's Soldier Field. Dempsey floored Tunney in the seventh round, but referee Dave Barry delayed starting the count until Dempsey retreated to a neutral corner. With at least five extra seconds to collect his wits, Tunney was able to regain his feet and eventually win the "Battle of the Long Count."

On May 6, 1921, Poland's Stanislaus Zbyszko, godson of the
renowned pianist Paderewski, defeated Ed "Strangler" Lewis in New
York City to win the World Heavyweight Wrestling Championship.

ig Bill Tilden, seen here practicing at Forest Hills, dominated men's tennis from 1920 to 1926. He was unbeatable in the U.S., won Wimbledon the two years he competed, and went 13–1 in singles matches in the Davis Cup challenge round.

hen Suzanne Lenglen of France (left) and America's Helen Wills met for the first time in 1926 at Cannes, the demand for tickets made scalpers rich. Lenglen won, 6–3, 8–6, but turned pro soon after and they never played each other again.

In a sport that let professionals and amateurs compete together in open tournaments, amateur Bobby Jones was a gallery favorite on both sides of the Atlantic. From 1923 to 1929 he won four U.S. Amateurs, three U.S. Opens, and two British Opens. And his greatest year was yet to come.

1930–1939

Jesse Owens stood head and shoulders above the competition at the Berlin Olympics of 1936.

1930–1939

1930

The stock market crash

of October 1929 marked the symbolic end of the Roaring Twenties, but it took four more years for the magnitude of the country's economic collapse to be realized. By 1933, the same year Prohibition was repealed, prices of industrial stocks had fallen by nearly 80 percent, close to 9,000 banks had failed, and millions of Americans had lost their life savings. The hard-charging optimism and prosperity of the Jazz Age had given way to the hard times of the Great Depression. ❧ **In sports,** an era ended in a Kansas wheat field on March 31, 1931, when 43-year-old Notre Dame football coach Knute Rockne was killed in a plane crash on his way to Los Angeles to make a football demonstration film. Rockne was the Golden Dome's gift to the Golden Age of Sport and one of nearly 22 million European immigrants who came to the United States between 1890 and 1930. He was five when his family arrived in America from Norway and settled in Chicago. Twenty years later he was an All-America end at Notre Dame as a senior and five years after that the head coach of the Fighting Irish. A renowned teacher, innovator, and promoter, he turned Notre Dame into America's favorite football team by playing the best schools in the land and winning 105 games and three national championships between 1918 and 1930. ❧

Another abrupt departure, although not a tragic one, was Bobby Jones' decision to retire from competitive golf at the height of his powers in 1930, just seven weeks after his unprecedented sweep of the open and amateur championships of the United States and Great Britain. Jones was just 28 when he won the Grand Slam and then walked away to concentrate on his real job as a lawyer in Atlanta. What made Jones unique was that he played only as an amateur, yet from 1923 to 1930 he dominated the

APR. 19
Clarence DeMar, who finished second in his first Boston Marathon in 1910, wins race for seventh time at age 41.

JUNE 12
In elimination final to determine successor to retired heavyweight champion Gene Tunney, Max Schmeling wins title on his back when a Jack Sharkey hook catches the German below his beltline in fourth round. Unable to continue, Schmeling is awarded title by disqualification.

JUNE 7
Gallant Fox wins Belmont Stakes, becoming only second three-year-old to win Preakness Stakes, Kentucky Derby, and Belmont in same year. Sportswriter Charles Hatton of the *Daily Racing Form* dubs the three events racing's "Triple Crown."

JULY 4
Helen Wills Moody wins her fourth straight Wimbledon singles championship a day before Bill Tilden wins his third singles title (and first since 1921) at Centre Court.

JULY 30
Host country Uruguay defeats Argentina, 4–2, in Montevideo to win first World Cup soccer championship.

SEPT. 17
Enterprise defeats challenger *Shamrock V* of Britain in four straight races to win first America's Cup challenge since 1920.

SEPT. 27
Bobby Jones trounces Gene Homans, 8 and 7, to win U.S. Amateur and complete first calendar-year sweep of golf's four major tournaments. He won British Amateur in May, British Open in June, and U.S. Open in July.

SEPT. 28
Chicago Cubs' Hack Wilson drives in his 189th and 190th runs of season in final game of year. New single-season record will remain untouched for remainder of century.

1931

FEB. 18
Bill Tilden makes his pro debut at Madison Square Garden, defeating Karel Kozeluh of Czechoslovakia in three sets before a crowd of 13,000.

JAN. 1
Unbeaten Washington State takes field in Rose Bowl game resplendent in bright red outfits from helmet to shoes but is trounced, 24–0, by unbeaten Alabama. The Crimson Tide and Notre Dame both go 10–0 and share national championship.

MAR. 31
Notre Dame football coach Knute Rockne is killed when a plane carrying him and seven others crashes in a Kansas wheat field. Rockne, who had coached the Fighting Irish since 1918, was 43.

JULY 6
Billy Burke defeats amateur George Von Elm by a stroke to win the longest playoff in U.S. Open history (72 holes). Burke is also first winner to use steel-shafted clubs.

AUG. 20
Helen Wills Moody wins singles title at U.S. Tennis Championships for seventh time in nine years.

OCT. 10
St. Louis Cardinals defeat Philadelphia A's, 4–2, in Game 7 of World Series. Cards' hero Pepper Martin, who has 12 hits, five stolen bases, and a .500 batting average in Series, is later named winner of first Associated Press male athlete of year award.

NOV. 12
Maple Leaf Gardens opens in Toronto, but 13,542 fans are disappointed when the Leafs lose to Chicago, 2–1. NHL's newest arena was built in 165 days at a cost of $1.5 million.

NOV. 21
Down 14–0 after three quarters, Southern California rallies to beat Notre Dame, 16–14, on a last-minute field goal at South Bend. The loss is first for the Irish in 26 games.

1932

JUNE 21
Challenger Jack Sharkey outpoints heavyweight champion Max Schmeling in controversial split decision in New York that results in Schmeling's American manager Joe Jacobs screaming the immortal words: "We wuz robbed!"

FEB. 15
First Winter Olympics held in United States end at Lake Placid with Americans winning most medals (12) and sweeping speed skating and bobsled races. Norway's Sonja Henie wins her second straight figure skating gold medal.

JUNE 25
Gene Sarazen wins U.S. Open with a tournament-record score of 286 two weeks after capturing British Open with a record 283. He is aided with his new invention, the sand wedge.

JULY 31
France defeats United States, 3–2, to win Davis Cup for sixth straight year.

OCT. 1
Babe Ruth homers into center field bleachers on "called" shot off Chicago Cubs pitcher Charlie Root in Game 3 of World Series. Visiting Yankees complete four-game sweep of Cubs the next day.

AUG. 14
Summer Olympics close in Los Angeles with U.S. dominating competition, but international participation is poor due to worldwide Depression. Games feature makeshift Olympic Village for men, automatic timing, photo-finish cameras, and victory platforms for medal winners. Sprinter Eddie Tolan and hurdler-javelin thrower Babe Didriksen of U.S. win two gold medals each.

DEC. 18
Chicago Bears defeat Portsmouth (Ohio) Spartans, 9–0, in playoff game to break tie for first place following NFL regular season.

1933

JAN. 13
Augusta National Golf Club, brainchild of Bobby Jones and architect Alister Mackenzie, officially opens outside Atlanta.

JUNE 10
Ralph Guldahl bogeys final hole, allowing amateur Johnny Goodman to win U.S. Open. Goodman will be last amateur to win the Open this century.

Korea's Sohn Kee-chung won the 1936 Olympic marathon running for Japan.

Don Budge

only sport where amateurs and professionals were allowed to mingle, winning four U.S. Opens and three British Opens. ❧ **Tennis had its first Grand Slam winner** in 1938 when America's Don Budge collected the national championships of Australia, France, England, and the United States. But since none of those tournaments was open to professionals (and wouldn't be for another 30 years), Budge was unable to test himself against the likes of Fred Perry, Ellsworth Vines, and the aging Bill Tilden until he turned pro in 1939. ❧ **The Depression forced sports,** especially the pros, to make do with less. Baseball attendance fell 40 percent from 1930 to 1933 before rebounding by the end of the decade. The woeful St. Louis Browns drew only 88,113 paying customers for the entire 1933 season and even fewer (80,922) in 1935, but none of the 16 major league teams folded. The National Football League and National Hockey League were not quite as stable—the NFL lost eight franchises but added six to end the decade with 10 teams, while the NHL dropped from 10 clubs to seven. ❧ **With many franchises barely hanging on,** some teams cut ticket prices, most cut salaries, and a few, like the Philadelphia A's, sold off their star players to keep from going under. The A's cashed in the nucleus of their 1929 and 1931 world championship teams— Al Simmons, Lefty Grove, Mickey Cochrane, and

Jimmie Foxx—for over $500,000 between 1932 and 1935. They finished last or second to last five years in a row, but they were solvent. The Cincinnati Reds introduced night games to the major leagues in 1935 and more than doubled their attendance. By the 1940s, every team in the majors was playing under the lights except the Chicago Cubs. ✌ *Chicago Tribune* **sports editor** Arch Ward, who had been Rockne's publicity aide at Notre Dame for the 1919 and 1920 football seasons, came up with two of the era's top promotions: producing the baseball All-Star Game in 1933 and following it up a year later with the Chicago College All-Star Game, which matched the defending National Football League champions against an all-star team of the past season's top college seniors. Both games featured fan voting for the all-star teams and both were immediate hits. ✌ **Chicago Stadium owner**

Sonja Henie

Arthur Wirtz experienced similar success in 1936 when he signed three-time Olympic figure skating gold medalist Sonja Henie for a staggering $150,000 a year to star in his International Ice Carnival. Meanwhile in New York, college basketball got a tremendous lift when promoter Ned Irish put on the first intersectional doubleheaders at Madison Square Garden during the 1934–35 season. Three years later, Irish organized the first National Invitational Tournament, which proved to be so successful the NCAA started a postseason playoff of its own in 1939. ✌ **College football attendance slumped** somewhat in the early thirties, but revived as major schools

JUNE 29
Italy's Primo Carnera, a 6'7", 260-pound former circus strongman, upsets heavyweight champion Jack Sharkey in sixth-round knockout at Long Island City, N.Y.

OCT. 1
Baseball regular season ends with Philadelphia sluggers Jimmie Foxx of the A's and Chuck Klein of the Phillies winning Triple Crowns and Yankees' Babe Ruth pitching a complete-game victory over Red Sox in final mound appearance of his career.

JULY 6
Baseball's first All-Star Game is held at Comiskey Park in conjunction with Chicago World's Fair. Two-run homer by 38-year-old Babe Ruth highlights American League's 4–2 victory over NL.

DEC. 17
Chicago Bears defeat New York Giants, 23–21, in first official NFL Championship Game between regular-season division winners.

1934

MAR. 25
Horton Smith beats Craig Wood by one stroke to win first Augusta National Invitational. Tournament started by Bobby Jones would soon be known simply as "the Masters."

MAY 28
Already the reigning world lightweight and junior welterweight champion, Barney Ross adds world welterweight title to his collection by dethroning Jimmy McLarnin in a 15-round split decision at Polo Grounds.

JULY 10
New York Giants pitcher Carl Hubbell strikes out American League sluggers Babe Ruth, Lou Gehrig, Jimmie Foxx, Al Simmons, and Joe Cronin in order during All-Star Game at Polo Grounds.

DEC. 9
Trailing unbeaten Chicago Bears 10–3 halfway through NFL Championship Game, the New York Giants don basketball shoes to improve their traction on frozen field at Polo Grounds. Giants rally to upset Bears, 30–13, in "Sneakers Game."

JUNE 14
Challenger Max Baer knocks down world heavyweight champion Primo Carnera 11 times before winning title by TKO in 11th round at Long Island City, N.Y.

OCT. 9
St. Louis Cardinals rout Detroit, 11–0, in Game 7 of World Series. In sixth inning, with St. Louis ahead 9–0, Commissioner Landis removes Cards left fielder Joe Medwick from game after Tigers fans shower Medwick with fruit and debris following his scuffle with Detroit third baseman Marv Owen.

DEC. 29
Madison Square Garden stages its first college basketball doubleheader. A crowd of 16,188 turns out to see Westminster (Pa.) beat St. John's, 37–33, and NYU defeat Notre Dame, 25–18.

1935

JAN. 1
Alabama beats Stanford, 29–13, in battle of undefeated teams at Rose Bowl. Tulane and Bucknell win first-ever Sugar and Orange bowls, respectively.

APR. 8
Double-eagle two on 485-yard 15th hole enables Gene Sarazen to tie Craig Wood after four rounds in second annual Masters tournament. Sarazen wins 36-hole playoff by five strokes the next day.

MAY 24
First night game played in major leagues at Cincinnati's Crosley Field. Crowd of 20,422 sees hometown Reds beat Philadelphia Phillies, 2–1.

MAY 25
Ohio State's Jesse Owens breaks five world records and equals a sixth at Big Ten track and field championships in Ann Arbor, Mich. Owens takes first place in 100-yard and 220-yard dashes, 220-yard low hurdles, and long jump.

MAY 25
Babe Ruth, now with Boston Braves, belts final three home runs of his career out of Forbes Field in Pittsburgh. He will retire from baseball on June 2.

JUNE 13
A year after winning world heavyweight championship, Max Baer loses his first title defense when he is outpointed by challenger James J. Braddock in Long Island City, N.Y.

JUNE 8
Jockey Willie Saunders rides Omaha to victory in Belmont Stakes to win racing's Triple Crown. Omaha's sire, Gallant Fox, won Triple Crown in 1930.

AUG. 31
Glenna Collett Vare wins her record-sixth U.S. Women's Amateur championship, 3 and 2 over 17-year-old Patty Berg.

OCT. 7
Detroit Tigers win first World Series ever, beating the Chicago Cubs four games to two.

DEC. 10
University of Chicago halfback Jay Berwanger receives first Downtown Athletic Club Trophy in New York. Award is renamed the Heisman Memorial Trophy in 1936 following death of D.A.C. athletic director and former college coach John Heisman.

1936

FEB. 2
New Baseball Hall of Fame announces that baseball writers have chosen Ty Cobb, Babe Ruth, Honus Wagner, Christy Mathewson, and Walter Johnson as charter members.

JAN. 1
Stanford, playing in its third consecutive Rose Bowl, beats top-ranked SMU, 7–0, on a first-quarter touchdown.

FEB. 11
Canada's dominance in Olympic hockey ends at Winter Games in Garmisch-Partenkirchen, Germany, where Great Britain beats Canadians, 2–1, and goes on to win gold medal. Norway wins 15 overall medals, including Sonja Henie's third straight gold in figure skating.

MAR. 24
Detroit beats Montreal Maroons, 1–0, in longest overtime game in NHL history. Red Wings' Mud Bruneteau finally scores at 16:30 of sixth overtime period in Game 1 of Stanley Cup semifinals. Detroit goes on to win series and its first-ever Cup.

British Open, St. Andrews, Scotland, 1933

Jay Berwanger

strengthened their schedules and the Associated Press began releasing a weekly poll of national sportswriters in 1936 that ranked the top 20 teams in the country. Postseason interest also picked up with the Sugar, Orange, and Cotton bowls joining the Rose Bowl on New Year's Day and the Downtown Athletic Club of New York presenting its first DAC Trophy, to University of Chicago halfback Jay Berwanger in 1935. The prize was renamed the Heisman Trophy a year later. ❧ Berwanger was also the first player selected in the NFL's inaugural college draft in 1936. Chosen by the Philadelphia Eagles, he was traded to the Chicago Bears, whose owner and head coach George Halas lost interest when Berwanger asked for a no-cut contract worth $25,000 over two years. Bronko Nagurski, the best player the Bears had and a three-time All-Pro fullback, was only making $5,000 a year. "Coach Halas," said Nagurski, "tossed nickels around like they were manhole covers." ❧ Nagurski, perhaps more than any pro athlete, epitomized the era. He was tough, straight ahead, and able to see the humor in hard times. America became a resourceful, opportunistic country during the Depression, and Nagurski, a native of International Falls, Minnesota, was as scrappy as they came. So were baseball players Pepper Martin and Dizzy Dean and the Gas House Gang in St. Louis. And so was Mildred "Babe" Didriksen, the best female athlete in the country and winner of two gold medals in track and field at the 1932 Summer Olympics in Los Angeles. ❧ Ty Cobb and Babe Ruth, the greatest hitter and slugger, respectively, in baseball history, were the top two votegetters in the 1936

Hall of Fame, opening day, 1939. Front row: Eddie Collins, Babe Ruth, Connie Mack, and Cy Young. Back row: Honus Wagner, Grover Cleveland Alexander, Tris Speaker, Nap Lajoie, George Sisler, and Walter Johnson.

balloting for the new Hall of Fame in Cooperstown, N.Y. Meanwhile, half a world away in Australia, cricket's greatest batsman ever, Don Bradman, was

Don Bradman

in the midst of a storied career in which he averaged 99.9 runs per test-match innings from 1928 to 1948. 🏏 But as the whirlwind of the Depression led to turmoil and the rise of Fascism in Europe, the most celebrated American athletes of the decade became Jesse Owens and Joe Louis—two young black men from Alabama who exposed the empty boast of Aryan supremacy. The 1936 Summer Olympics in Berlin and the two heavyweight fights between Louis and former German world champion Max Schmeling at Yankee Stadium in 1936 and 1938 served as the preliminaries to the United States and Germany slugging it out in World War II. 🏏 Owens came to Berlin a year after causing a sensation at the 1935 Big Ten track and field championships, where in one afternoon he broke five world records and tied a sixth. This time out he won an unprecedented four gold medals in seven days, eliciting chants of "Yes-sa O-vens! Yes-sa O-vens!" that rivaled the "Sieg Heils" Hitler received from the daily crowds that filled the 110,000-seat Olympic Stadium. Hard-pressed to explain Owens' success and the additional nine medals won by his nine black

MAY 30
Louis Meyer wins Indianapolis 500 for third time in nine years. Californian's average speed of 109.069 mph is fastest in 25-year-old event.

JULY 3
Fred Perry wins third straight Wimbledon singles title, but he will be last Englishman to win championship for remainder of century.

DEC. 1
The Associated Press winds up first season of weekly Top 20 college football poll by naming Minnesota as national champion. Gophers have 23–1 record over last three seasons.

JUNE 19
Former heavyweight champion Max Schmeling, 30, stuns boxing world by knocking out unbeaten 22-year-old Joe Louis in 12th round of their non-title bout at Yankee Stadium in New York.

AUG. 3
Jesse Owens of U.S. wins 100-meter gold medal at Summer Olympics in Berlin. He will also win the 200 meters, long jump, and run first leg of 4 x 100-meter relay for an unprecedented four gold medals.

1937

JAN. 1
Quarterback Sammy Baugh leads Texas Christian to 16–6 victory over Marquette in first Cotton Bowl game at Dallas.

FEB.13
Two months after moving the Boston vs. Green Bay NFL Championship Game to the Polo Grounds in New York, Boston Redskins owner George Preston Marshall moves club to his hometown of Washington, D.C.

MAR. 8
Howie Morenz, Montreal Canadiens star and the NHL's top gate attraction, dies of a heart attack at age 34 while recovering in hospital from a leg fracture.

MARCH
Center jump after each score is eliminated in college basketball and each team is given 10 seconds to advance ball past center-court line.

JUNE 5
War Admiral wins Belmont Stakes to become third Triple Crown-winning horse of decade. Jockey is Charley Kurtsinger.

JUNE 21
Two years after becoming world heavyweight champion, James J. Braddock is knocked out in first title defense. He falls in eighth round to Joe Louis at Chicago's Comiskey Park.

JULY 20
Don Budge of U.S. rallies from two sets down to beat Gottfried von Cramm of Germany, 6–8, 5–7, 6–4, 6–2, 8–6, in Davis Cup interzone final at Wimbledon. Budge's win, called by some the "greatest tennis match ever played," gains America a 3–2 victory and berth in challenge round against defending champion Great Britain. U.S. beats Britain, 4–1, a week later.

OCT. 10
Yankees beat Giants, four games to one, in second straight all-New York World Series.

DEC. 11
Former world heavyweight wrestling champion Strangler Lewis announces his retirement at age 47 and criticizes the sport for becoming "slam-bang" entertainment featuring heroes, villains, and fixed matches.

1938

MAR. 16
Temple routs Colorado, 60–36, to win first National Invitation Basketball Tournament at Madison Square Garden. Byron (Whizzer) White scores 10 points for Colorado 10 weeks after scoring eight points and throwing touchdown pass in 28–14 loss to Rice in Cotton Bowl.

JUNE 15
Johnny Vander Meer of Cincinnati becomes first major league pitcher to throw consecutive no-hitters, blanking Brooklyn, 6–0, in first night game at Ebbets Field. Four days before, he no-hit the Boston Braves, 3–0. Four days later, the Braves' Debs Garms ended Vander Meer's bid for three in a row with a fourth inning single.

JULY 2
Helen Wills Moody, 32, beats American arch-rival Helen Jacobs, 30, in straight sets to claim her record eighth Wimbledon singles tennis title. Meeting is their 11th with Moody enjoying a 10–1 edge, including wins in all four of their Wimbledon finals.

SEPT. 24
Don Budge defeats doubles partner Gene Mako in four sets to win U.S. Tennis Championship and become first player to sweep all four major titles—Australian, French, British, and American—in one calendar year. Budge, 23, will turn pro before year is out.

APR. 12
Bill Stewart, who is a National League baseball umpire during NHL off-season, becomes first American-born hockey coach to win Stanley Cup when his Chicago Black Hawks beat Toronto, three games to one.

JUNE 21
Heavyweight champion Joe Louis avenges only loss of his pro career by knocking out Max Schmeling in first round. A crowd of 70,000 sees rematch at Yankee Stadium while millions more listen in on radio.

AUG. 17
Henry Armstrong wins 15-round split decision over world lightweight champion Lou Ambers in New York to become only fighter to hold featherweight, lightweight, and welterweight titles simultaneously.

OCT. 9
New York Yankees sweep Chicago Cubs, becoming first team to win three consecutive World Series titles.

NOV. 1
Match race between 1937 Triple Crown winner War Admiral and five-year-old Seabiscuit ends with Seabiscuit winning by three lengths before record-crowd of 43,000 at Pimlico Race Course in Baltimore.

1939

JAN. 15
First Pro Bowl All-Star Game played at Wrigley Field in Los Angeles with NFL champion New York Giants defeating All-Stars, 13–10.

MAY 2
New York Yankees first baseman Lou Gehrig benches himself "for the good of the team," ending his consecutive-game playing streak at 2,130.

MAR. 27
Oregon defeats Ohio State, 46–33, to win first National Collegiate men's basketball tournament at Evanston, Ill. Started by the National Association of Basketball Coaches, tourney will be taken over by NCAA in 1940.

JUNE 11
Byron Nelson out-shoots Craig Wood, 70–73, to win U.S. Open in second 18-hole playoff after both golfers card 68s in first 18 holes.

42nd running of Boston Marathon, 1938

teammates, the Nazis criticized the United States for relying on "black auxiliaries." ❧ **Two months earlier,** before his first bout with Louis, Schmeling had been criticized for demeaning the white race by fighting a black man (and an undefeated one at that). When Schmeling upset Louis with a 12th-round knockout, he was quickly embraced by the Nazis as a paragon of Teutonic manhood. ❧ **In the rematch,** Louis entered the ring carrying the weight of the free world on his shoulders. He was world champion now, having taken the title from James J. Braddock the year before, and, for the first time in the nation's history, America was rooting for a black man against a white challenger. And it wasn't just because Schmeling was a Nazi. Louis' handlers had taken great care from the start of his career to avoid any comparisons to Jack Johnson, the former black champion who had been loathed by white Americans. ❧ **With 75,000 looking on** at Yankee Stadium and another 70 million listening on the radio, Louis demolished Schmeling in 124 seconds. Wrote New York *World-Telegram* columnist Heywood Broun the next day: "One hundred years from now some historian may theorize, in a footnote at least, that the decline of Nazi prestige began with a left hook." ❧

Schmeling–Louis rematch

On July 30, 1930, Uruguay and Argentina met in Montevideo in the final of the first World Cup. Down 2–1 at intermission, Uruguay came back in the second half to win the game on this deciding goal by Santos Iriarte. In Montevideo, Uruguayans rejoiced. In nearby Buenos Aires, a mob of angry Argentines stoned the Uruguayan consulate.

With his wins in the sprints, long jump, and 400-meter relay, all the Master Race could do with Jesse Owens at the Berlin Olympics was keep track of his gold medals.

Babe Didriksen elbows her way to a two-inch victory over teammate Evelyn Hall in the 80-meter hurdles final at the 1932 Olympics in Los Angeles. Didriksen also won the javelin and took second in the high jump. In 1950, an Associated Press poll ranked her as the greatest female athlete of the half-century.

Seabiscuit was a late-bloomer. After two unsuccessful campaigns he came into his own as a four-year-old and won Horse of the Year honors in 1938 at age five. His biggest victory that year came in a November 1 match race at Pimlico with 1937 Triple Crown winner War Admiral. Seabiscuit, on the rail, not only won by three lengths but set a record for a mile and a sixteenth.

French rider Maurice Archambaud leads Learco Guerra of Italy into the Parc des Princes velodrome. This one-lap sprint would determine the final-stage winner of the 1933 Tour de France.

When heavy snows made it impossible to use Wrigley Field as a playoff site to break a first-place tie at the end of the 1932 season, Chicago Bears owner George Halas booked a hockey arena instead. On December 18, the Bears and Portsmouth (Ohio) Spartans faced off at Chicago Stadium on an 80-yard field of dirt left behind by the circus. The Bears won the game, 9–0, on a disputed touchdown pass from Bronko Nagurski to Red Grange. But the unique playing conditions led to several important rules changes—the NFL's first break from college rules—including instituting hash marks on the field, legalizing forward passes from anywhere behind the line of scrimmage, and moving the goalposts from the back of the end zone to the goal line.

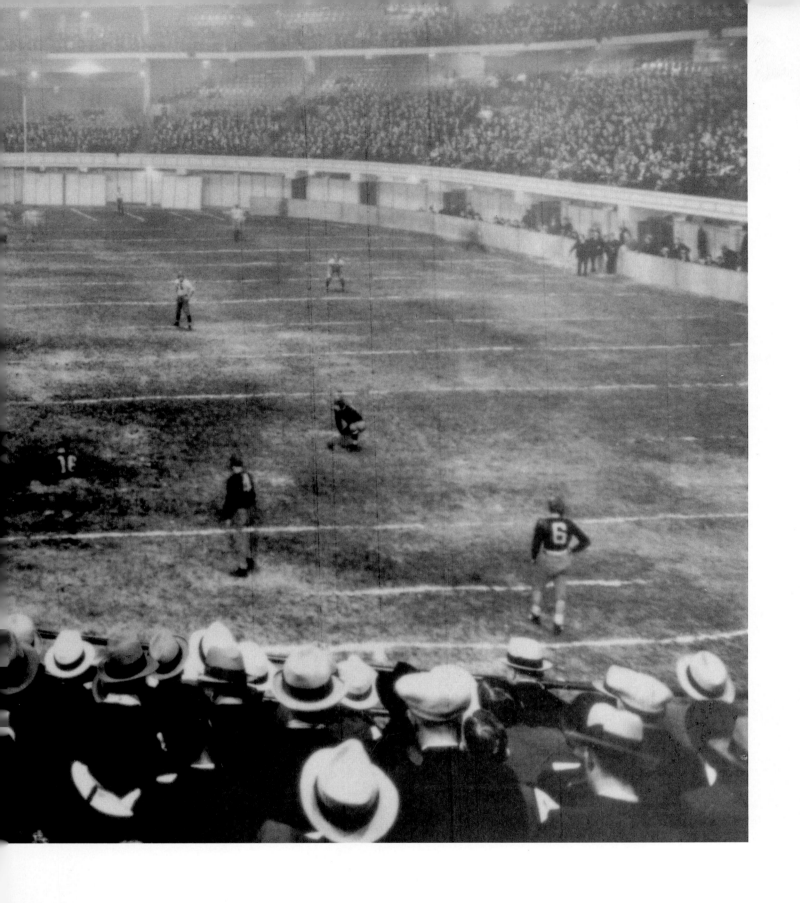

The 1939 Rose Bowl was resolved on this 14-yard touchdown pass from fourth-string Southern Cal quarterback Doyle Nave to reserve end Al Krueger with 41 seconds left. USC won the game, 7–3, over a Duke squad that had entered the contest undefeated, untied, and unscored upon.

The NFL played its first scheduled championship game between division winners at Wrigley Field on December 17, 1933. Three field goals by helmetless Jack Manders helped the Chicago Bears beat the New York Giants, 23–21, in a seesaw battle that saw the lead change hands six times.

The Americans were New York's first NHL hockey team and shared Madison Square Garden with the more successful Rangers from 1926 until they folded in 1942. This is one of hockey's earliest indoor game action shots.

Harold Larwood of England bounces a ball past the head of Australia's Bill Woodfull in the fourth test at Brisbane, March 15, 1933. The English strategy of bowling directly at the batters—giving the series the nickname "bodyline"—sparked a diplomatic crisis that saw Australia threaten to break ties with Great Britain and withdraw from the Commonwealth.

Lou Gehrig had played in 2,130 consecutive games until May 2, 1939, in Detroit, when he asked his manager, Joe McCarthy, to bench him. "I felt I wasn't helping the club by the way I was playing," he said. Afterwards he watched his teammates take the field.

This photo is a baseball classic. Mickey Cochrane, the most acrobatic of catchers, has taken the throw, spun around, and, in an improbable relation to gravity, elegantly intercepted the runner. Who needs ballet?

In the years before telephoto lenses, photographers worked in foul ground to capture action shots that make today's generation of lensmen pine for the good old days. The Nijinsky imitator is Earl Averill.

On May 25, 1935, in Pittsburgh, Babe Ruth hit the final three home runs of his glorious career. In a snapshot taken from the stands, he rounds third for the last time. Above, a few days later, he is portrayed in a pensive moment; only he knows it is his final game.

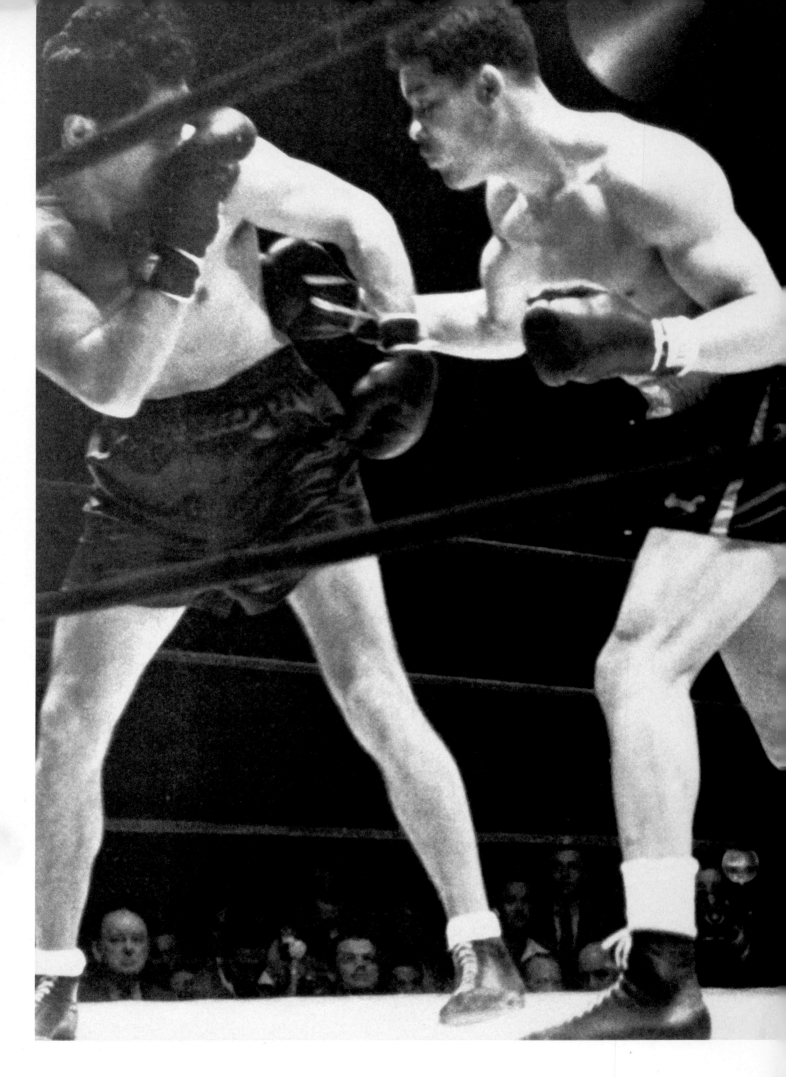

In 1936 Max Schmeling knocked out undefeated Joe Louis in the 12th round of a nontitle bout. Two summers later, in the first round of their rematch, Louis, now heavyweight champion, landed a terrific right to the kidney that made Schmeling scream; the knockout followed. Louis did not lose again in this decade or the next.

1940–1949

Philadelphia Eagles' bench braves blizzard during 1948 title game.

1940–1949

Six days after Japan

attacked Pearl Harbor on December 7, 1941, the United States Army directed the governor of California to cancel the New Year's Day Tournament of Roses Parade and the Rose Bowl game between Oregon State and Duke. Any and all large gatherings on the West Coast, said the Army, presented an unacceptable public safety risk given the proven aggressiveness of the enemy. ❧ The Tournament of Roses Association received two invitations to relocate the game: one from *Chicago Tribune* sports editor Arch Ward, who could deliver 120,000-seat Soldier Field as the alternate playing site, and the other from Duke head coach Wallace Wade, who offered a more modest stadium in Durham, North Carolina, that held 35,000, but could be enlarged to 52,000 by adding temporary stands. Wade sent Oregon State athletic director Percy Locey a telegram that said Duke was prepared to make good on its offer, "with Rose Bowl sanction or otherwise." ❧ Wade got the game, but Duke lost, 20–16. The Rose Bowl returned to Pasadena the following year when the tide had turned against the Japanese in the Pacific, but its temporary change of address was minor compared to the outright cancellation of many national and international sporting events during the seven years of World War II. ❧ The dominoes started to fall in 1938 when Japan quit as host of the 1940 Winter and Summer Olympics a year after its invasion of China. Although the International Olympic Committee tried to reschedule the Games in Europe, the outbreak of hostilities on the continent in 1939 forced the IOC to abandon the idea and eventually to call off the 1944 Olympics as well. As long as war raged, annual international competitions from Wimbledon tennis to World Cup

1940

FEBRUARY
Winter and Summer Olympic Games, originally scheduled for Sapporo and Tokyo, Japan, are canceled due to outbreak of World War II in 1939.

JULY
British Open golf and tennis championships at Wimbledon canceled for duration of World War II.

DEC. 8
Visiting Chicago Bears administer record 73–0 shellacking to Washington Redskins in NFL Championship Game. Bears score 11 touchdowns and outrush Redskins 381 to 5.

APR. 13
New York Rangers beat Toronto, four games to two, to win third Stanley Cup in 13 years. It will be 54 years until they win their fourth Cup.

OCT. 8
Cincinnati beats Detroit in seven games to win first World Series since the scandal-plagued victory against Chicago White Sox in 1919.

1941

JAN. 1
Stanford, featuring first-year coach Clark Shaughnessy's modern T-formation offense, beats Nebraska, 21–13, in Rose Bowl. Victory completes greatest one-season turnaround in NCAA history: from 1–7–1 for 1939 season to 10–0–0 in 1940.

JUNE 7
Whirlaway, with Eddie Arcaro aboard, wins Belmont Stakes to become fifth horse to win racing's Triple Crown.

JUNE 18
Ahead on points after 12 rounds in his heavyweight championship fight with champion Joe Louis, Billy Conn ignores advice from his corner and goes for a knockout in the 13th round. He is knocked out by Louis instead before a crowd of 54,486 at Polo Grounds.

JULY 17
Indians pitchers Al Smith and Jim Bagby and third baseman Ken Keltner (two great defensive plays) combine to stop Joe DiMaggio's record hitting streak at 56 games before crowd of 60,000 in Cleveland.

SEPT. 28
Entering final day of regular season with batting average of .3995, Boston's Ted Williams goes 6-for-8 in doubleheader against Philadelphia A's to end season at .406.

OCT. 5
Dropped third strike by Dodgers catcher Mickey Owens with two outs in ninth inning costs Brooklyn chance to even World Series with Yankees after four games. New York wins Game 5 the next day to wrap up ninth Series in 19 years.

1942

JAN. 15
President Franklin Roosevelt gives Major League Baseball "green light" to continue playing during war.

JAN. 1
Three and a half weeks after Pearl Harbor, Rose Bowl game is moved to Durham, N.C., where Oregon State upsets previously undefeated Duke, 20–16. Game will return to Pasadena in 1943.

Baseball went to war.

OCT. 5
Underdog St. Louis Cardinals beat Yankees in five-game World Series.

APR. 18
Toronto Maple Leafs defeat Detroit, 3–1, to win Stanley Cup. Leafs are first team in history of Cup final to lose first three games then win next four.

DEC. 1
Ohio State, coached to a 9–1 record by 34-year-old Paul Brown, is voted national champion in the season's final AP writers Top 20 poll.

1943

APR. 1
NCAA tournament champion Wyoming upsets NIT champ St. John's, 52–47, in Red Cross benefit game at Madison Square Garden.

APR. 7
NFL allows Cleveland Rams to suspend operations for a year. Two months later, Philadelphia and Pittsburgh permitted to merge rosters for coming season. Team will be known as "Steagles."

JUNE 5
Count Fleet, Johnny Longden up, wins Belmont Stakes by 25 lengths to capture racing Triple Crown.

OCT. 11
Yankees win 10th World Series title, taking rematch with Cardinals in five games. Cards make 10 errors.

NOV. 27
Notre Dame is denied an undefeated season when Great Lakes (Ill.) Naval Training Station beats the Irish, 19–14, with only 33 seconds left in their final game. Final AP Top 20 poll still names Notre Dame No. 1.

DEC. 26
Quarterback Sid Luckman throws record five touchdown passes as Chicago Bears beat Washington Redskins, 41–21, for third NFL title in four years.

1944

FEBRUARY
Winter and Summer Olympic Games, originally scheduled for Cortina d'Ampezzo, Italy, and London, are canceled due to continuation of World War II.

MAR. 28
Utah's "Blitz Kids" (average age: 18) beat veteran Dartmouth squad, 42–40, to win NCAA championship at Madison Square Garden. Two nights later at the Garden, Utes beat NIT champ St. John's, 43–36, in Red Cross benefit game.

APRIL
NFL permits Pittsburgh and Chicago Cardinals to merge rosters for the coming season. "Card-Pitt" goes 0–10 and earns nickname of "Carpets."

OCT. 1
St. Louis Browns beat Yankees, 5–2, to clinch first pennant in franchise history on last day of regular season. Sellout crowd at Sportsman's Park is Browns' first in 20 years.

soccer were put on hold. 🍂 **Spared the widespread destruction** suffered by much of Europe and Asia, the United States shook off the last effects of the Depression and reduced the unemployment rate to one percent by retooling its manufacturing plants and producing extraordinary amounts of war materials for the fight against Japan and Germany. Fifteen million American men entered the service, including a majority of the country's professional and amateur athletes. 🍂 **Following a spectacular 1941** season in which Joe DiMaggio hit safely in 56 straight games, Ted Williams batted .406, and the Brooklyn Dodgers won their first pennant in 21 years, Commissioner Kenesaw Mountain Landis wrote to President Franklin Roosevelt offering to shut the game down for the duration of the war if the president wished. Roosevelt replied with his "green light" letter of January 15, 1942, saying, "I honestly feel it would be best for the country to keep baseball going." FDR expected all players of military age to go into the service, but added, "Even if the actual quality of the teams is lowered by the greater use of older players, this will not dampen the popularity of the sport." 🍂 **He was right.** By 1945 major league attendance was over 10 million for the first time since 1930 despite rosters dotted with old-timers, draft rejects, underage kids, a one-armed

Sammy Baugh, back to pass, 1942 NFL Championship Game

St. Louis Browns outfielder named Pete Gray, and a one-legged Washington pitcher named Bert Shepard. Still, as had been the case since 1884, there was no room in major league baseball for able-bodied black players; such stars as Satchel Paige, Josh Gibson, and Oscar Charleston continued to play in that shadow land of organized baseball, the Negro Leagues.

❧ For the National Football League, the public's attention to the modern T-formation as it developed in Chicago in 1939 and the Bears' 73–0 annihilation of Washington in the 1940 championship game gave way to lean times during the war years. Rosters and coaching staffs were so depleted that the Cleveland Rams opted to suspend operations in 1943, the Pittsburgh Steelers were allowed to combine rosters with the Philadephia Eagles in 1943 (the "Steagles") and the Chicago Cardinals in 1944, and the Brooklyn Tigers had to merge with the Boston Yanks in 1945. The National Hockey League also lost a team, the New York Americans, making the NHL a six-team operation as of the 1942–43 season. ❧ With few exceptions, star players entering the military continued to play ball for service teams. Recruiting battles between base commanders was often intense, especially in football, where many of the best college players and coaches were drafted off one campus and sent to either a base or another campus that had war-related flight-training programs. The talent in some of those programs was so good their football teams were ranked in the weekly Associated Press Top 20 poll. In 1943, for instance, Iowa Pre-Flight, coached by Missouri's Don Faurot, had the second-ranked team in the country after Notre Dame, while former Ohio State coach Paul Brown's Great Lakes Naval Training Station squad was ranked sixth. ❧ The end of the war in 1945 was followed in short

OCT. 9
Only All-St. Louis World Series of century ends with Cardinals defeating Browns in six games. Browns make 10 errors.

DEC. 2
No. 1 Army beats No. 2 Navy, 23–7, in final game of season for both teams. Led by sophomore backs Doc Blanchard and Glenn Davis, Cadets march through schedule averaging 56 points per game.

1945

MAR. 18
Montreal Canadiens third-year right winger Maurice (Rocket) Richard becomes first NHL player to score 50 goals in a season, which is only 50 games long.

MAR. 29
NCAA champion Oklahoma A&M, starring 7-foot Bob Kurland, beats NIT champ DePaul, starring 6-foot-10 George Mikan at Madison Square Garden. Aggies win Red Cross benefit game, 52–44.

JULY 1
Less than two months after Germany's surrender in Europe, Detroit Tigers first baseman Hank Greenberg is released from Army and homers in first game back. Most other major leaguers in service will return in 1946.

JULY 10
All-Star Game scheduled for Fenway Park canceled because of wartime travel restrictions. Instead, seven inter-league benefit games are played during All-Star break.

AUG. 19
Byron Nelson's 11-tournament PGA winning streak ends at Memphis Invitational where he finishes fourth. Record run includes year's only major, the PGA. Nelson will end season with 18 victories and $63,336 in prize money, both records.

OCT. 10
Detroit beats Chicago Cubs, 9–3, in Game 7 to win second World Series in 11 years. For Cubs, this Series appearance will be their last for remainder of century.

DEC. 1
Army (8–0) and Navy (7–0–1) meet for second year in row as top two-ranked teams in the nation. Army wins again, 32–13.

DEC. 16
Cleveland Rams edge Washington Redskins, 15–14, to win their first NFL Championship Game. On Jan. 12, 1946, NFL will allow Rams to move to Los Angeles.

1946

MAR. 26
Oklahoma A&M beats North Carolina, 43–40, in NCAA tournament final, becoming first team to repeat as national collegiate basketball champions.

JAN. 1
Sophomore quarterback Bobby Layne of Texas runs for four touchdowns, throws for two more and kicks four extra points as Longhorns beat Missouri, 40–27, in Cotton Bowl.

JUNE 2
Assault, with Warren Mehrtens in the saddle, wins Belmont to become third Triple Crown-winning horse of decade.

JULY 5
Sam Snead, one of the few American golfers to make the trip, wins first British Open since 1939 by four strokes on Old Course at St. Andrews.

SEPT. 1
Patty Berg wins inaugural U.S. Women's Open, beating Betty Jameson, 5 and 4, in match-play event.

SEPT. 20
New All-America Football Conference opens first season with Paul Brown's Cleveland Browns routing Miami Seahawks, 44–0, before crowd of 60,135 in Cleveland.

OCT. 15
St. Louis Cardinals capture third World Series in five years, beating Boston Red Sox in Game 7 when Enos Slaughter scores winning run from first base on Harry Walker double in bottom of eighth inning.

NOV. 1
Visiting New York Knicks defeat Toronto Huskies, 68–66, in opening game of new 11-team Basketball Association of America. BAA will merge with rival National Basketball League in 1949.

NOV. 9
No. 1 Army and No. 2 Notre Dame bring unbeaten records and explosive offenses to Yankee Stadium and play to a scoreless tie. Three weeks later, Army is denied third straight national championship when final AP writers poll ranks Irish (8–0–1) first and Cadets (9–0–1) second.

DEC. 15
Chicago Bears beat New York Giants, 24–14, at Polo Grounds to claim fourth NFL championship in seven seasons. After the game Giants Frank Filchock and Merle Hapes are suspended indefinitely for failing to report bribe offer to lose game by more than 10 points.

DEC. 22
Cleveland Browns defeat New York Yankees, 14–9, to win inaugural All-America Football Conference championship game.

1947

MAR. 24–25
Madison Square Garden hosts back-to-back college basketball championship games in front of standing-room-only crowds. Utah upsets Kentucky, 49–45, for the NIT championship one night, and Holy Cross rallies to beat Oklahoma by 11 the next.

APR. 10
Brooklyn Dodgers purchase Jackie Robinson's contract from their Montreal farm club making Robinson first black player in major leagues. Five days later, he will debut at first base and go 0-for-3 against Boston Braves.

APR. 19
In first all-Canadian Stanley Cup final in 12 years, Toronto Maple Leafs defeat Montreal Canadiens in six games.

APR. 22
Philadelphia Warriors win first BAA title, beating Chicago Stags, four games to one, in finals.

Al Gionfriddo robs Joe DiMaggio, 1947 World Series

AAFC action, 1948

order by the return of American soldiers from overseas and the start of the postwar baby boom. Sports boomed, too. In 1946 alone, Major League Baseball attendance jumped 80 percent, the number of professional football teams grew to 18 with the creation of the All-America Football Conference (AAFC), and pro basketball found itself with two leagues and 23 teams. ❧ **The AAFC was another Arch Ward brainstorm,** born in 1944 of millionaire owners who couldn't gain entrance to the NFL and the belief that pro football was ripe for expansion south and west. The league lasted only four seasons, but nurtured two franchises, the four-time champion Cleveland Browns and the San Francisco 49ers, that would go on to greater glory after joining the NFL in 1950. After an absence of black players in pro football since 1933, two teams with Cleveland in common signed two blacks each in 1946. The NFL Rams, who left Cleveland for Los Angeles after the 1945 season, suited up former UCLA teammates halfback Kenny Washington and end Woody Strode, while Cleveland's newest team, the AAFC Browns, debuted fullback Marion Motley and guard Bill Willis. Motley and Willis made All-AAFC as rookies in 1946, the year before Jackie Robinson reached the major leagues in baseball. ❧ **Desegregation of the armed forces** during the war, even if on a trial basis, gave momentum to the process that would eventually integrate big-league baseball. The death of Commissioner Landis in 1944 and the election of former Kentucky governor Happy Chandler to take his place also helped. Landis had long opposed letting blacks play, while Chandler, to the surprise of many given his segregationist

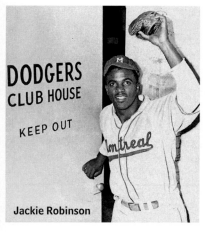

DODGERS
CLUB HOUSE
KEEP OUT

Jackie Robinson

background, had no objections. ❧ **That opened the door** for Brooklyn Dodgers president Branch Rickey to sign Robinson, the 28-year-old, former four-sport star at UCLA, army second lieutenant, and infielder with the Kansas City Monarchs. The pressure on Robinson to succeed was enormous. Rickey had chosen him to break baseball's color line because his character and self-control matched his prowess on the field. And Robinson came through, withstanding the taunts of opposing players and fans and leading the Dodgers to National League pennants as Rookie of the Year in 1947 and Most Valuable Player in 1949. ❧ **Newspapers deemed Robinson's breakthrough** a great day for baseball and race relations in America, but it was also the death knell for the Negro Leagues. The eventual migration of black players to the major leagues would kill what was one of the prime black-managed businesses in the country. ❧ **While Branch Rickey was busy** trying to get black players into Major League Baseball, Harlem Globetrotters owner Abe Saperstein was just as determined to keep blacks out of both the National Basketball League and the Basketball Association of America. The barnstorming Globetrotters, who played an entertaining up-tempo game, were the most exciting team in pro basketball and had the attendance figures to prove it. Saperstein also had a monopoly on the best black talent and wanted to keep it that way. ❧ **But integration was inevitable.** In 1948, the Globetrotters split two exhibition games with 6-foot-10 George Mikan and the NBL champion Minneapolis Lakers. Two seasons later, the NBL and

JULY 19
Babe Didriksen Zaharias wins Colorado Springs golf tournament for 17th consecutive victory, including the 1946 U.S. Women's Amateur and the '47 British Women's Amateur. She will turn pro in August.

SEPT. 14
Wimbledon champion Jack Kramer rallies from two sets down to beat Frank Parker in final of U.S. Tennis Championships at Forest Hills. Kramer turns pro after tournament.

OCT. 6
Yankees beat Dodgers in seventh and deciding game of World Series.

NOV. 2
Ryder Cup matches between U.S. and Britain resume in Portland, Ore., after 10-year layoff due to war. With players like Hogan, Nelson, and Snead among others, Americans win easily, 11–1.

DEC. 5
In battle of 33-year-olds, Joe Louis barely holds on to his world heavyweight championship in a 15-round split decision over Jersey Joe Walcott at Madison Square Garden.

DEC. 9
Notre Dame and Michigan both go 9–0 during regular season, but final AP Top 20 poll names Irish number-one team in country.

DEC. 12
Bill France meets with other southeastern race promoters at Daytona, Fla., to form the National Association for Stock Car Auto Racing (NASCAR).

DEC. 26
A crowd of 15,114 braves snowstorm to fill Madison Square Garden for Jack Kramer's professional tennis debut against pro champ Bobby Riggs. Riggs wins in four sets.

1948

MAY 30
Driver Mauri Rose wins Indianapolis 500 for second year in a row and third time in last four races dating back to 1941, when he shared his ride with Floyd Davis. Rose joins Wilbur Shaw and Louie Meyer as only three-time champions.

JULY 3
Louise Brough wins singles, doubles, and mixed doubles titles at Wimbledon, becoming only third woman to claim all three in same year. Suzanne Lenglen and Alice Marble are the others.

JAN. 30
First Olympic Games in 12 years get underway in St. Moritz, Switzerland, with 28 nations represented, but Germany and Japan barred as wartime aggressors. U.S. gold medalists include 18-year-old figure skater Dick Button, alpine skier Gretchen Fraser, and four-man bobsled team.

JUNE 12
Citation wins Belmont Stakes, becoming fourth three-year-old of decade to capture racing's Triple Crown. Eddie Arcaro, who rode another Calumet Farm horse Whirlaway in 1941, becomes only jockey to win Triple Crown twice.

JULY 29
First post-war Summer Olympic Games open in London. Germany and Japan not invited, but a record 59 countries participate.

AUG. 6
Seventeen-year-old Bob Mathias of California becomes youngest gold medalist in Olympic men's track and field history when he wins the decathlon.

OCT. 10
Led by manager-shortstop and American League MVP Lou Boudreau, Cleveland Indians win first World Series since 1920, eliminating Boston Braves in six games.

NOV. 30
Final AP Top 20 poll ranks Michigan (9–0) and Notre Dame (9–0–1) first and second in nation.

1949

FEB. 2
Ben Hogan is critically injured when his car collides head-on with a bus. While doctors originally feared he might not walk again, Hogan recovered and was back out on tour in 11 months.

FEB. 7
New York Yankees make Joe DiMaggio baseball's first $100,000 a year player.

MAR. 1
Joe Louis relinquishes heavyweight championship after reign of 11 years, eight months, and 25 successful defenses.

APR. 13
Minneapolis Lakers defeat Washington Capitols in six games to win BAA championship. During summer, league will merge with remainder of NBL and become new, 17-team National Basketball Association.

JUNE 22
Ezzard Charles gains unanimous 15-round decision over Jersey Joe Walcott in Chicago in fight to fill vacant world heavyweight championship.

JULY
Gussie Moran of the U.S. causes a sensation at staid Wimbledon by wearing lace-trimmed panties under her tennis skirt.

DEC. 3
Notre Dame beats SMU, 27–20, to finish season undefeated for fourth year in a row. Over that time the Irish forged a 35–0–2 record and won three AP national titles.

DEC. 11
Cleveland Browns win fourth AAFC championship in four years, beating San Francisco 49ers, 21–7. Two days before game the NFL announced AAFC was folding and Browns, 49ers, and Baltimore Colts would join NFL in 1950.

DEC. 18
Philadelphia wins second straight NFL title game in lousy weather. In 1948 the Eagles beat the Chicago Cards, 7–0, in a snowstorm. This time they beat the Los Angeles Rams, 14–0, in the pouring rain.

Bob Mathias winning Olympic decathlon, London 1948

BAA merged to become the NBA. And a year after that, ex-Globetrotter Sweetwater Clifton was one of the three initial blacks to play in the NBA. ❧ **The Olympic games resumed in 1948** after a 12-year lapse, almost as an afterthought of a world at war. Germany and Japan were not invited to either the Winter Games in St. Moritz or the Summer Games in London, which the Luftwaffe had tried to flatten during the Battle of Britain. Fanny Blankers-Koen, a 30-year-old Dutch mother of two, was the star of the London Games, winning four gold medals in track and field. Back in 1936, the highlight of her first Olympics in Berlin had been coming home with Jesse Owens' autograph. ❧ **Finally, in the forties America** sat down and watched sports on television. As usual, Major League Baseball, college football, and boxing were immediate hits, but so were sports like roller derby and professional wrestling, which women found to be more entertaining and TV programmers relished because they could be

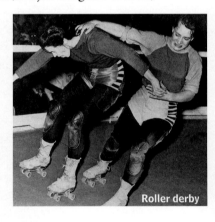
Roller derby

managed to conform with evening viewing schedules. ❧ **One of the new medium's first celebrities** was a trash-talking pro wrestler named George Wagner, who billed himself as Gorgeous George, wore his peroxided hair in ringlets, favored white boots and satin quilted robes, and was always attended by a valet whose duties included deodorizing the ring with eau de toilette spray. ❧ **While the World Series** was first broadcast on TV in 1947, the first Emmy Award given for sports programming went to KTLA in Los Angeles in 1949 for its coverage of pro wrestling. ❧

Fifteen different Chicago players scored in the Bears' 73–0 rout of the Washington Redskins in the 1940 NFL Championship Game. This 68-yard touchdown run by fullback Bill Osmanski was the second play of the game.

The Cleveland Browns were champions of the All-America Football Conference in each season of its four-year existence (1946–49). The Browns' Marion Motley (right) was the AAFC's most fearsome running back.

Chicago Cardinals quarterback Paul Christman hurries a pass against Washington on a muddy Sunday afternoon at Griffith Stadium. In 1947 the Cards' "dream backfield" of Christman, Charley Trippi, Elmer Angsman, and Pat Harder (34) led the franchise, since removed to St. Louis and then Phoenix, to its only Championship Game victory.

Byron Nelson won a record 18 tournaments in 1945, including a staggering 11 straight from the Miami Four-Ball in March to the Canadian Open in August. The wartime competition was inconsistent, but Nelson's individual brilliance was not.

Bowling-alley fun had its sadistic side in the days before automatic pin-setters.

Willie Mosconi was the greatest pool player ever, a 14-time world champion from 1941 to 1957, but as the sport declined in popularity he was often reduced to exhibition play in nowhere venues.

A huge crowd watches a preliminary bout at Yankee Stadium before the second Joe Louis–Billy Conn fight on June 19, 1946. Outdoor fights are today an anachronism.

Early in 1940, Chilean Arturo Godoy fought Joe Louis for the heavyweight title and lost a 15-round split decision. That led to a rematch four months later, but this time Godoy only lasted eight rounds.

By expert consensus, Sugar Ray Robinson remains the greatest fighter of the century, pound for pound. In his 26-year career in the ring he fought 202 times and knocked out 109 opponents, including the unfortunate Cecil Hudson, twice.

The man on the canvas is Sid Goldstein, and he is staring up at the lights of St. Nick's Hall in New York, where the hopes of aspiring palookas had run into left hooks since 1905.

For two days in mid-August 1948, Babe Ruth's body lay in state at Yankee Stadium. More than 200,000 fans paid their last respects.

In 1941 Ted Williams (above, left) and Joe DiMaggio (above) provided baseball with two landmark achievements. Williams hit .406, becoming the last man in the century to break the .400 barrier. Joe D, here shown cracking a hit in his 56th straight game, set a mark that survived the century.

Jockey Eddie
Arcaro works out
Citation during the
three-year-old's
Triple Crown
campaign in 1948.
Arcaro also rode
Whirlaway to the
Triple Crown
in 1941.

If the hallmark of 20th century sports is speed, the ancient sport of bocce would seem a likely casualty—yet somehow it retains its appeal.

From the standpoint of a spectator, nothing—neither horse racing nor auto racing—conveys the sensation of pure, exhilarating speed like six-day bike racers coming around the banked boards of a velodrome.

Here is pro basketball below the rim, and nearly beneath notice. In the early years of the National Basketball Association, the Zollner Pistons played their home games at North Side High School in Ft. Wayne, Indiana. The gym, which could host up to 3,800 fans for an NBA game—like this one against the Syracuse Nationals— was a far cry from where the Detroit Pistons play today, at the Palace of Auburn Hills.

In the late 1940s the best basketball was not necessarily played in the NBA. AAU teams like the Phillips 66ers, starring former

Oklahoma All-American Bob Kurland, or barnstorming clubs like the Harlem Globetrotters could give the league boys a real tussle.

Americans, who dominated Olympic diving from 1920 to 1936, picked up where they left off at the postwar Summer Games in London, as Sammy Lee swept the platform and springboard events.

Twelve years after Jesse Owens won four track and field gold medals at the Berlin Olympics, 30-year-old Fanny Blankers-Koen of Holland won four races at the London Games, including the first-ever women's 200 meters.

The first Olympics held after World War II were the 1948 Winter Games at St. Mortiz, Switzerland, where 18-year-old Dick Button became the first American to win a gold medal for figure skating.

1950–1959

City College of New York vs. St. John's at Madison Square Garden in 1950

1950–1959

Not many Americans

knew what a point spread was until a 1951 criminal investigation into sports gambling by New York District Attorney Frank Hogan revealed that between 1947 and 1950 some 86 college basketball games in 23 cities had been fixed by 32 players from seven colleges. ❧ Unbelievably, the two schools in the middle of the scandal had won the last two NCAA championships—Kentucky in 1949 and City College of New York in 1950. Seven CCNY players confessed to taking money (up to $3,000) in return for either dumping games or shaving points so that the Beavers would win by a closer score than the line set by bookmakers. Former Kentucky All-Americas Alex Groza and Ralph Beard, who led the Wildcats to two NCAA titles, won gold medals as members of the 1948 United States Olympic team, and were now first team All-Stars in the NBA, also admitted shaving points for money. As a result, the Southeastern Conference suspended Kentucky for the 1953 season and the NBA banished Groza and Beard for life. ❧ The point spread came to the attention of gamblers in the late thirties when Chicago bookmaker Charles McNeil popularized the idea that wagering on team sports would be much more appealing to bettors if a margin of victory was set between two unequal teams rather than relying on the old racetrack-based odds system. The spread, or line, soon became the handicap of choice in sports betting and would prove to be the engine behind the rise of pro football as the country's most popular sport. ❧ Meanwhile, another outrage unearthed by Hogan's investigation showed that some colleges had forged academic records to get unqualified students admitted and then kept them eligible with a steady diet of cupcake courses. Like the game-fixing disclosures, it was

1950

MAR. 19–28
City College of New York beats Bradley twice in 10 days to win both NIT and NCAA basketball championships at Madison Square Garden. CCNY ends season with record of 24–5.

APR. 23
Pete Babando's goal in double overtime of Game 7 gives Detroit Red Wings a 4–3 victory over New York Rangers in Stanley Cup final.

JUNE 19
Uruguay beats Brazil, 2–1, to win first soccer World Cup since 1938. Upset of tournament in Argentina is the United States' 1–0 victory over England in first round.

JUNE 10
Sixteen months after a near-fatal car accident, Ben Hogan reestablishes himself as the world's top golfer by winning a three-way playoff to claim his second U.S. Open title.

SEPT. 27
Attempt by former heavyweight champion Joe Louis to regain title falls short as current champion Ezzard Charles wins unanimous 15-round decision at Yankee Stadium.

SEPT. 16
Four-time AAFC champion Cleveland Browns whip NFL champion Philadelphia Eagles, 35–10, in opening game of NFL season.

OCT. 7
Purdue snaps Notre Dame's 39-game unbeaten football streak, beating Irish 28–14.

OCT. 1
Babe Zaharias wins U.S. Women's Open to complete sweep of all three major titles on new Ladies Professional Golf Association tour. She won the Titleholders in March and Western Open in June.

DEC. 24
Cleveland Browns beat Los Angeles Rams, 30–28, on last-second Lou Groza field goal to add NFL championship to four straight AAFC titles.

OCT. 7
Philadelphia Phillies, who won their first NL pennant in 35 years, are swept from World Series by New York Yankees.

1951

JAN. 1
Seventh-ranked Kentucky upsets No. 1 Oklahoma, 13–7, in Sugar Bowl, ending Sooners' unbeaten season.

FEB. 18
Three members of CCNY basketball team that won NIT and NCAA titles in 1950 are arrested in New York for fixing college games. Investigations reveal players from six other colleges, including Kentucky, are involved.

JULY 18
Jersey Joe Walcott, a two-time loser in heavyweight championship fights with Joe Louis and Ezzard Charles, finally wins title at age 37, knocking out Charles in seventh round at Pittsburgh's Forbes Field.

AUG. 19
Measuring just 3-foot-7, midget Eddie Gaedel of Bill Veeck's St. Louis Browns walks on four pitches against Detroit in only at bat. The following day, an unamused AL president Will Harridge voids Gaedel's contract.

SEPT. 4
Sixteen-year-old Maureen Connolly becomes youngest woman to win U.S. singles title at Forest Hills, beating Shirley Fry in three sets.

SEPT. 12
Sugar Ray Robinson, who lost his middleweight title to unsung Briton Randy Turpin on July 10, regains it by knocking Turpin out in 10th round of their rematch at Polo Grounds.

OCT. 10
Bubble bursts for Giants in all-New York World Series where AL champion Yankees win their third consecutive title.

OCT. 3
New York Giants win playoff for NL pennant when Bobby Thomson hits three-run homer off Dodgers' Ralph Branca in bottom of ninth inning of deciding game. Second place Giants trailed Dodgers by 13 1/2 games on Aug. 11.

1952

JAN. 24
Ted Rhodes, Bill Spiller, and amateur Eural Clark play in Phoenix Open under new PGA rule allowing blacks to enter tournament if sponsor agrees.

FEB. 29
Dick Button captures his fifth consecutive world figure skating championship a week after winning his second straight Olympic gold medal.

FEB. 14
Winter Olympics open in Norway, birthplace of modern skiing. Local hero, however, turns out to be speed skater Hjalmar Andersen who wins three gold medals. American champions include alpine skier Andrea Mead Lawrence who wins twice.

MAR. 23
Chicago right wing Bill Mosienko scores fastest hat trick in NHL history with three goals in 21 seconds against New York Rangers at Madison Square Garden.

JULY 19
Summer Olympics open in Helsinki, Finland, with Soviet Union participating for first time ever. USSR will finish close second to U.S. in overall medals, 76–71.

JULY 27
Czechoslovakia's Emil Zatopek wins Olympic marathon in Helsinki, completing unprecedented sweep of 5,000-meter, 10,000-meter, and marathon gold medals. Zatopek had never run a marathon before.

SEPT. 23
Unbeaten challenger Rocky Marciano knocks out heavyweight champion Jersey Joe Walcott in 13th round before crowd of 40,379 in Philadelphia.

OCT. 7
Down three games to two, Yankees come back to beat Dodgers in seven games for fourth straight World Series championship.

DEC. 28
Former Dallas high school teammates Bobby Layne and Doak Walker lead Detroit Lions to first NFL championship in 17 years, beating Cleveland Browns, 17–7.

1953

MAR. 18
National League owners unanimously approve Boston Braves' petition to move franchise to Milwaukee for 1953 season.

JAN. 11
Baltimore granted expansion team by NFL. Team will be named Colts, same as old AAFC team that lasted only one season in NFL in 1950.

Bobby Layne led Detroit to NFL titles in 1952 and 1953.

Cliff Hagan of Kentucky

nothing new, but was shocking nonetheless. In the end, some of the players and bribers behind the fixes were sent to jail and the NCAA championship game was withdrawn from Madison Square Garden, long a haven for big-city gamblers. ✒ **Similar to baseball's recovery** in the wake of the Black Sox scandal three decades before, college basketball came back from disgrace with the 1951 appointment of no-nonsense administrator Walter Byers as the NCAA's first full-time executive director, the decision to televise the NCAA tournament, and the arrival of exciting new players like Bill Russell, Wilt Chamberlain, Elgin Baylor, Oscar Robertson, and Jerry West. Memorable games like North Carolina's 54–53 triple-overtime victory against Chamberlain and Kansas in the 1957 NCAA final didn't hurt, either. ✒ **America in the fifties** was a country on the move—the migration of the middle class from the cities to the suburbs, the building of the interstate highway system, the introduction of coast-to-coast jet airline service, and the population drift from the North and Midwest to the South and the West, thanks in no small measure to advances in air conditioning. ✒ **Baseball was still the country's dominant sport,** but by the end of the 1952 season attendance was down over 30 percent from a postwar high of 21 million in 1948. One problem was the growing availability of games on television, which generated additional revenue from networks and local stations but cut deeply into the live gate. The impact of TV during the decade also made regional or rural teams much less attractive and led to a severe

Giants welcome Bobby Thomson home.

reduction in existing minor leagues, from 59 to 20 over the course of the decade. Another drawback was that the major leagues hadn't budged an inch in 50 years, with 16 teams in 10 cities and no outpost west of St. Louis or south of Washington, D.C. At the beginning of the decade, four cities had two teams each and New York had three. By 1959 only Chicago would have two clubs. 🌢 **The three teams with the fewest** paying customers all moved from 1953 to 1955: the Boston Braves to Milwaukee, the St. Louis Browns to Baltimore, and the Philadelphia A's to Kansas City. But the biggest change of address came in 1958 when the Dodgers and Giants, baseball's best rivalry, left worn-out ballparks in New York City for the untapped goldfields of California. The recent memories of Bobby Thomson's "Shot Heard 'Round the World" in 1951, the Willie Mays catch off Vic Wertz in the 1954 World Series, and the Dodgers' first world championship in 1955 were now suddenly ancient history. 🌢 **While only 653,923 fans** had come to watch the Giants finish sixth in their last season at the Polo Grounds, the Dodgers had drawn over a million fans to Ebbets Field for the 13th year in a row. Walter O'Malley, who had succeeded the crusading Branch Rickey as part-owner and team president in 1950, was making a tidy profit in Brooklyn but recognized he could make a killing in Los Angeles. 🌢 **"O'Malley was the**

MAY 29
Edmund Hillary of New Zealand and Tenzing Norgay of Nepal are first two men to reach top of Mount Everest and return. Everest is world's highest mountain at 29,028 feet.

OCT. 5
New York Yankees become first team to win World Series five years in a row, eliminating Brooklyn in six games.

NOV. 9
U.S. Supreme Court rules 7–2 that baseball is a sport, not a business, and thus not subject to antitrust laws.

JULY 10
Ben Hogan wins British Open at Carnoustie, Scotland, becoming first golfer to win Masters, U.S. Open, and British Open in same calendar year. He passed up PGA Championship (July 1–7) to practice for only British Open appearance of his career.

SEPT. 7
Eighteen-year-old Maureen Connolly beats Doris Hart, 6–2, 6–4, to win U.S. Championships at Forest Hills and complete first women's tennis Grand Slam.

OCT. 24
Notre Dame ends Georgia Tech's 31-game unbeaten streak with 27–14 victory in South Bend. Coach Frank Leahy collapses at halftime and retires after season with career record of 107–13–9 and winning percentage (.864) second only to Knute Rockne.

1954

MARCH
Making first appearance on international hockey scene, Soviet Union wins world championship tournament in Sweden. Russians rout Canada, 7–2, in tournament final.

JULY 3
Fifteen months after undergoing surgery for colon cancer, Babe Didriksen Zaharias wins third U.S. Women's Open by 12 strokes.

JULY 4
West Germany defeats Hungary, 3–2, to win World Cup final in Bern, Switzerland.

JAN. 1
Fourth-ranked Oklahoma upsets No. 1 Maryland, 7–0, in Orange Bowl. Game marks third time in four years top-ranked team has fallen in bowl game.

MAY 6
Roger Bannister, a 25-year-old medical student, breaks four-minute mile barrier with time of 3:59.4 at Oxford, England.

SEPT. 17
A bloody Rocky Marciano rallies in the eighth round to knock out Ezzard Charles and hold on to his world heavyweight championship. Bout comes three months after Marciano scored a unanimous 15-round decision over Charles.

OCT. 2
New York Giants beat Cleveland in four straight games to win their first World Series since 1933. Sweep comes after Indians set major league record with 111 regular-season victories.

OCT. 30
NBA opens 1954–55 season with a 24-second clock to limit a team's possession of the ball without taking a shot; another new rule limits teams to six fouls per quarter.

1955

FEB. 22
Unhappy with progress of her rehabilitation from horse-riding accident in July, 20-year-old Maureen Connolly announces her retirement from tennis after winning nine major singles championships in last four years.

MAY 30
Looking to become the first driver to win three consecutive Indianapolis 500s, Bill Vuckovich, 36, is killed in a five-car collision while leading the race after 140 miles.

AUG. 31
Nashua, the Preakness and Belmont champion, meets Swaps, the Kentucky Derby winner, in a $100,000 winner-take-all match race at Washington Park in Chicago.

SEPT. 21
Defending his heavyweight title for last time, undefeated Rocky Marciano knocks out light heavyweight champion Archie Moore in ninth round at Yankee Stadium.

OCT. 4
Brooklyn Dodgers win their first World Series in eight attempts as Johnny Podres blanks Yankees, 2–0, in Game 7.

NOV. 28
Oklahoma is named national champion in the final AP Top 20 poll after fourth undefeated regular season in seven years.

DEC. 9
Sugar Ray Robinson, 35, who gave up his middleweight title in 1952 to enter show business, regains the crown with a second-round knockout of champion Bobo Olson at Chicago Stadium.

DEC. 26
Cleveland Browns beat Los Angeles Rams, 38–14, to win third NFL title since joining league in 1950. Quarterback Otto Graham retires after leading team to 10 straight AAFC and NFL title games and winning seven of them.

1956

FEB. 5
Winter Olympics end in Cortina d'Ampezza, Italy, with Soviet Union winning most medals in their debut at the Winter Games. Austria's Toni Sailer sweeps men's alpine events and Tenley Albright becomes first U.S. woman to win figure skating gold medal.

MAR. 24
Led by center Bill Russell, undefeated San Francisco beats Iowa, 83–71, to win second straight NCAA basketball title. Russell will also lead U.S. Olympic team to gold medal in Melbourne in fall.

SEPT. 9
Ken Rosewall ends Lew Hoad's grand slam quest at Forest Hills. Hoad falls one championship short as Davis Cup doubles partner beats him in four sets for U.S. title. Rosewall turns pro, Hoad doesn't.

SEPT. 27
Babe Zaharias, female athlete of the half-century and star of the LPGA golf tour, dies at age 42 after a long bout with cancer.

NOV. 30
Floyd Patterson, 21, becomes youngest heavyweight champion ever by knocking out a man twice his age, Archie Moore, in fifth round of their Chicago bout to succeed Rocky Marciano.

DEC. 3
Final AP Top 20 poll puts Oklahoma on top again as Sooners run unbeaten streak to 40.

Don Larsen's perfect game, 1956 World Series

first to say out loud that it was business," wrote columnist Red Smith years later, "a business that he owned and could operate as he chose, and the community the team had pretended to represent for almost 70 years had no voice in the matter at all. From that day on, some of the fun of baseball was lost." ✒

Pro basketball became fun again during the 1954–55 NBA season when stalling was eliminated by the adoption of the 24-second clock. The brainchild of Syracuse Nationals owner Danny Biasone, the 24-second clock set a limit on the time a team had to get a shot off after gaining possession of the ball. "I never claimed to be an expert on the game," said Biasone, "but I knew fans weren't paying to see the ball dribbled around all night." ✒ **The clock and a new rule** limiting each team to six fouls per quarter tilted the balance of power in the pro game toward offense, with more running and much more scoring. The season before the 24-second clock was introduced, a typical NBA game saw two teams score a total of 159 points. By the 1959–60 season, that average was up 45 percent to 230.6 points a game. ✒ **Although the Minneapolis Lakers** were as close as pro basketball came to a dynasty in the fifties, with four NBA championships, they fell short of the Montreal Canadiens' five Stanley Cups, the New York Yankees' six World Series titles, and Australia's 8–2 record over the United States in Davis Cup challenge rounds. Meanwhile, in college football, the University of Oklahoma went unbeaten for 47 consecutive games from 1953 to 1957, and boxing's Rocky Marciano retired as the

Bud Wilkinson, Oklahoma coach

Sugar Ray Robinson vs. Gene Fullmer, 1957

undefeated heavyweight champion of the world in 1955, with a career record of 49–0 over nine years. Sugar Ray Robinson lost five fights in the fifties, but won the middleweight title a record five times from temporary holders Jake LaMotta, Randy Turpin, Bobo Olson, Gene Fullmer, and Carmen Basilio. 🐦

But over a 12-year period, from 1946 to 1957, no one could match the 11 championship game appearances of Paul Brown's Cleveland Browns. Four-time champions of the All-America Football Conference, the Browns joined the NFL a year later, beat the defending champion Philadelphia Eagles on opening day, and then won three NFL titles in the next six years. 🐦 **Brown succeeded because** he was better organized and more innovative than anyone else. He was the first coach to hire a year-round coaching staff, script an opening sequence of plays, use "messenger guards" to send in

Browns' Otto Graham vs. L.A. Rams, 1950

1957

DEC. 8
Despite American gold rush in men's track and field, Soviet Union dominates men's and women's gymnastics and wins most medals at Summer Olympics in Melbourne, Australia.

DEC. 30
New York Giants move from Polo Grounds to Yankee Stadium to start season, then end it at home with 47–7 victory over Chicago Bears to win first NFL title since 1938.

MAR. 23
Top-ranked North Carolina beats Wilt Chamberlain and No. 2 Kansas, 54–53, in triple-overtime to capture first NCAA basketball title.

APR. 13
Bill Russell and Boston Celtics win first NBA championship with double-overtime, 125–123 victory over St. Louis in Game 7 of NBA finals.

MAY 1
After losing his middleweight title to Gene Fullmer by decision in New York on Jan. 2, Sugar Ray Robinson wins it back four months later by knocking Fullmer out in fifth round in Chicago.

MAY 28
National League owners approve moves of Brooklyn Dodgers to Los Angeles and New York Giants to San Francisco provided they move to the West Coast together.

SEPT. 8
After becoming the first black player to win a singles title at Wimbledon in July, 30-year-old Althea Gibson of Harlem, N.Y., becomes the first black to win a singles title at Forest Hills.

SEPT. 23
Welterweight champion Carmen Basilio steps up to challenge Sugar Ray Robinson at Yankee Stadium and wins the title in a furious 15-rounder that ends up a split decision.

OCT. 5
Great Britain wins Ryder Cup for first time in 24 years, besting America's golf pros, 7 1/2 to 4 1/2, at Lindrick G.C. in Yorkshire, England.

OCT. 10
Milwaukee Braves win World Series as pitcher Lew Burdette registers third complete-game victory over New York Yankees in Game 7.

NOV. 16
The longest winning streak in college football history ends at 47 as visiting Notre Dame beats No. 1 Oklahoma, 7–0, in Norman. The Irish were 18-point underdogs.

DEC. 15
Cleveland rookie fullback Jim Brown leads NFL in rushing with 942 yards in 12 games. He will be the league's top rusher eight of the nine seasons he plays through 1965.

1958

MAR. 15
NBA playoffs open with Detroit Pistons meeting the Cincinnati Royals in a best-of-three series. Both clubs played elsewhere in 1957: the Pistons in Ft. Wayne, Indiana and the Royals in Rochester, N.Y.

MAR. 25
Sugar Ray Robinson, 36, wins middleweight title for fifth time, going distance against 30-year-old champion Carmen Basilio and taking a split decision.

APR. 6
Arnold Palmer eagles par-five 13th hole at Augusta to win Masters by a stroke, gaining first major victory at age 28.

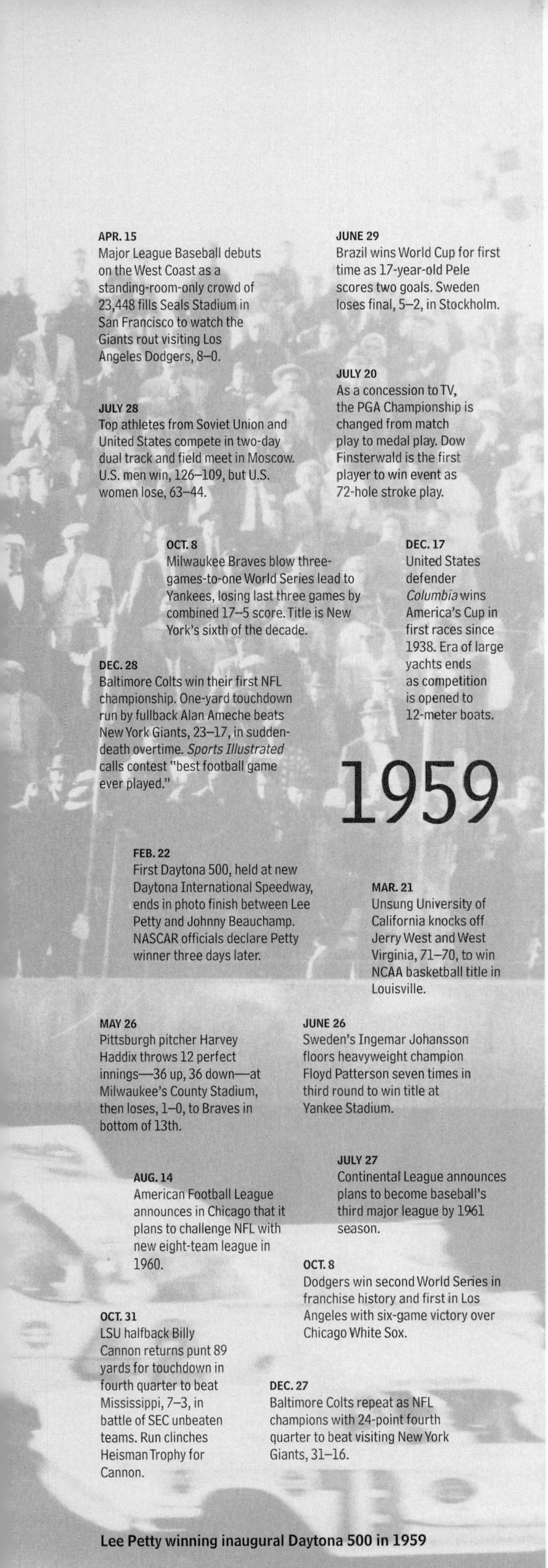

APR. 15
Major League Baseball debuts on the West Coast as a standing-room-only crowd of 23,448 fills Seals Stadium in San Francisco to watch the Giants rout visiting Los Angeles Dodgers, 8–0.

JUNE 29
Brazil wins World Cup for first time as 17-year-old Pele scores two goals. Sweden loses final, 5–2, in Stockholm.

JULY 20
As a concession to TV, the PGA Championship is changed from match play to medal play. Dow Finsterwald is the first player to win event as 72-hole stroke play.

JULY 28
Top athletes from Soviet Union and United States compete in two-day dual track and field meet in Moscow. U.S. men win, 126–109, but U.S. women lose, 63–44.

OCT. 8
Milwaukee Braves blow three-games-to-one World Series lead to Yankees, losing last three games by combined 17–5 score. Title is New York's sixth of the decade.

DEC. 17
United States defender *Columbia* wins America's Cup in first races since 1938. Era of large yachts ends as competition is opened to 12-meter boats.

DEC. 28
Baltimore Colts win their first NFL championship. One-yard touchdown run by fullback Alan Ameche beats New York Giants, 23–17, in sudden-death overtime. *Sports Illustrated* calls contest "best football game ever played."

1959

FEB. 22
First Daytona 500, held at new Daytona International Speedway, ends in photo finish between Lee Petty and Johnny Beauchamp. NASCAR officials declare Petty winner three days later.

MAR. 21
Unsung University of California knocks off Jerry West and West Virginia, 71–70, to win NCAA basketball title in Louisville.

MAY 26
Pittsburgh pitcher Harvey Haddix throws 12 perfect innings—36 up, 36 down—at Milwaukee's County Stadium, then loses, 1–0, to Braves in bottom of 13th.

JUNE 26
Sweden's Ingemar Johansson floors heavyweight champion Floyd Patterson seven times in third round to win title at Yankee Stadium.

JULY 27
Continental League announces plans to become baseball's third major league by 1961 season.

AUG. 14
American Football League announces in Chicago that it plans to challenge NFL with new eight-team league in 1960.

OCT. 8
Dodgers win second World Series in franchise history and first in Los Angeles with six-game victory over Chicago White Sox.

OCT. 31
LSU halfback Billy Cannon returns punt 89 yards for touchdown in fourth quarter to beat Mississippi, 7–3, in battle of SEC unbeaten teams. Run clinches Heisman Trophy for Cannon.

DEC. 27
Baltimore Colts repeat as NFL champions with 24-point fourth quarter to beat visiting New York Giants, 31–16.

Lee Petty winning inaugural Daytona 500 in 1959

plays, and utilize intelligence tests for evaluating personnel. He also introduced the draw play, the sideline pass, and the two-minute drill. And to run his sophisticated T-formation offense he had Otto Graham, a first team All-America in both football and basketball at Northwestern, and the only Big Ten tailback to beat Ohio State twice in the three seasons Brown coached the Buckeyes from 1941 to 1943. ❧ Weeb Ewbank, a Cleveland assistant who was hired by the Baltimore Colts in 1954 to assemble a Paul Brown-type team, found a quarterback even better than Graham when he signed Johnny Unitas as a free agent in 1956. Two years later, on December 28, 1958, the Colts met the New York Giants at Yankee Stadium for the NFL championship. With a nationwide television audience of nearly 11 million homes looking in on NBC, Unitas mortally wounded baseball as the national pastime by marching the Colts to a dramatic, game-tying, 20-yard field goal in the final two minutes and then engineering a 13-play, 80-yard touchdown drive to win the game after eight minutes of overtime. ❧ Four-year-old *Sports Illustrated* called it simply "The Best Football Game Ever Played." TV coverage in the New York metropolitan area had been blacked out and the city was in the grip of an 18-day newspaper strike, but Madison Avenue got the message: the NFL has arrived; stay tuned. ❧ It had taken the NFL 39 years to finally arrive, after its birth in a Hupmobile showroom in 1920. In 1952, the Soviet Union emerged from hibernation to rejoin the Olympic movement at the Summer Games in Helsinki—35 years after the Russian Revolution and 13 years after invading Finland during World War II. The return of the USSR turned the Olympics into a Cold War rivalry with the United States that would last until the collapse of communism in 1991. ❧

One year after losing the 1957 NCAA championship game to North Carolina in triple overtime, junior Wilt Chamberlain and Kansas were denied a return trip to the playoffs when Kansas State beat them for the Big Seven title.

Bob Pettit was the NBA's most decorated player in the fifties. He broke in with the Milwaukee Hawks as Rookie of the Year in 1954–55, won a pair of MVP awards in St. Louis after the team moved there, and led the Hawks to the NBA title in 1958, defeating the Boston Celtics in six games.

Into the boards! Gordie Howe (9) led the Detroit Red Wings to four Stanley Cups in the fifties, was the NHL's leading scorer five times, and won four Hart Trophies as the NHL's most valuable player. However, he never won the Lady Byng Trophy, awarded for sportsmanship and gentlemanly conduct.

oronto Maple Leafs defenseman Bill Barilko won the 1951 Stanley Cup on this shot, a backhander over Montreal goaltender Gerry McNeil's shoulder at 2:53 in overtime of Game 5. It remains the only Stanley Cup Final series in which every game ended in overtime. It proved to be Barilko's last goal, as he died in a plane crash three months later.

Sixteen months after a near-fatal car accident had doctors wondering if he would ever walk again, Ben Hogan used a one-iron for his approach to the 72nd hole at Merion and then tied for the lead of the U.S. Open. The next day he shot 69 to win a three-way playoff.

Babe Didriksen Zaharias, the biggest draw in women's golf, reacts to a sluggish putt at the 1953 All-American Open in Chicago where she finished 15th just three and a half months after major cancer surgery. A year later she won her third U.S. Open, by 12 strokes.

In February 1958, most of the players for Manchester United, the top soccer team in the world, were killed in a plane crash in Munich (right). One of those who survived was Bobby Charlton (above), who went on to become arguably England's greatest player ever.

Althea Gibson (far left) was the first black player to win at Wimbledon and Forest Hills. Maureen Connolly (near left) was the first woman to win the Grand Slam. Above, their quarterfinal match at Forest Hills in 1953.

One of the century's breakthrough moments in sports came on May 6, 1954, at Iffley Road track in Oxford, where 25-year-old English medical student Roger Bannister broke the four-minute barrier in the mile with a time of 3:59.4. *Sports Illustrated* first appeared three months later and made Bannister its first "Sportsman of the Year" in December.

John Davis was a one-man weightlifting dynasty, going undefeated from 1938 until 1953. He won 11 national championships, six world titles, and gold medals in both the 1948 and 1952 Olympics, where he was never beaten in the press, the snatch, or the jerk.

Jackie Robinson steals home in the eighth inning of Game 1 of the 1955 World Series. The surprise theft energized the Brooklyn Dodgers as they went on to win their first and, as it turned out, only world championship.

In Game 1 of the 1954 World Series, with the score tied, Cleveland had two men on base when slugger Vic Wertz hit a fly to deepest center field. It landed in the glove of Willie Mays, "the place," an opponent said, "where triples go to die."

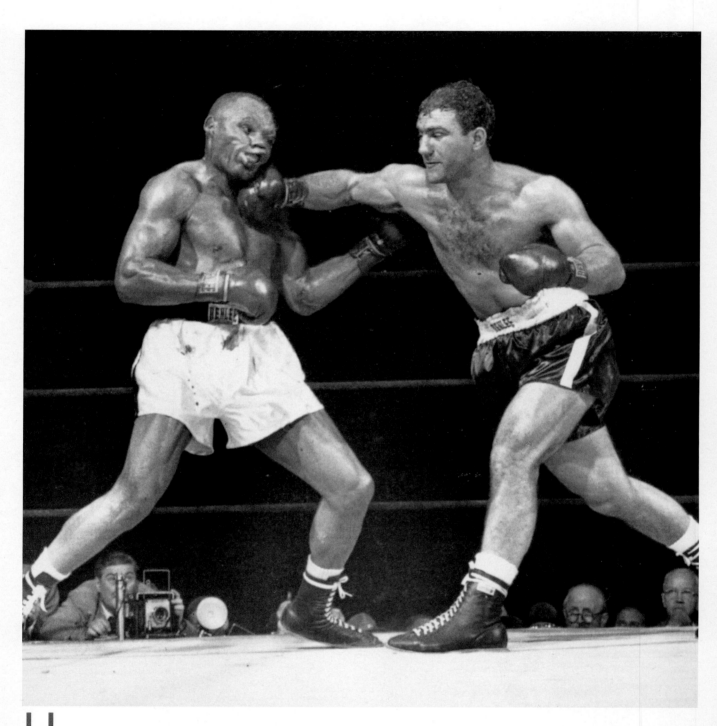

Here is the most famous single punch in boxing history. Trailing on all three cards after 12 rounds, Rocky Marciano fires a straight right that catches heavyweight champion Jersey Joe Walcott flush on the jaw. Walcott hit the floor and was counted out.

Hy Peskin was the great sports photographer of the era. This is one of his classics, a Carmen Basilio knockout of Tony DeMarco at Boston Garden, November 30, 1955.

1960–1969

A barefoot Abebe Bikila of Ethiopia wins the marathon at the Rome Olympics in 1960.

1960–1969

In 1960 Pete Rozelle

became commissioner of the National Football League, Lamar Hunt was founder and president of the brand new American Football League, Arnold Palmer won the Masters and the U.S. Open in golf, ABC-TV hired Roone Arledge as a sports producer, and Cassius Clay won the light-heavyweight gold medal in boxing at the Summer Olympics. Rozelle was 33 years old, Hunt 29, Palmer 30, Arledge 28, and Clay 18. ✒ **When you talk about sports** in the sixties, you start with these five young men. ✒ **Pete Rozelle** was a curious choice to succeed Bert Bell as commissioner when NFL owners elected him on the 23rd ballot the night of January 26, 1960. A compromise candidate, he was general manager of the Los Angeles Rams and not very good at it, given the Rams' 2–10 record. A blockbuster deal he made in 1959 that sent nine of his players to the Chicago Cardinals for running back Ollie Matson ended up hurting both teams and helped condemn the Rams to seven consecutive losing seasons. ✒ **Bell, who had been** one of the NFL's guiding lights since he came up with the idea of an annual college draft in 1935, had died the previous October of a heart attack suffered at an Eagles–Steelers game in Philadelphia. After his election as commissioner in 1944, he came down hard on gambling threats to the league, successfully turned back a costly challenge to the NFL by the All-America

Pete Rozelle

Football Conference, absorbed three AAFC teams in a merger, and presided over the league's rise in national popularity by embracing television but insisting that all home games be blacked out. ✒

1960

JAN. 26
NFL owners elect 33-year-old Pete Rozelle as new commissioner.

FEB. 25–28
U.S. Olympic hockey team beats Canada, Soviet Union, and Czechoslovakia over four days to win gold medal at Winter Games in Squaw Valley, Calif.

MAR. 19
Ohio State routs defending NCAA champion California, 75–55, to win national basketball championship in San Francisco.

APRIL 14
Montreal Canadiens sweep Toronto from Stanley Cup final to win unprecedented fifth straight title.

JUNE 18
Arnold Palmer, who won second Masters in April, fires final-round 65 to beat 20-year-old amateur Jack Nicklaus by two strokes at U.S. Open in Denver.

JUNE 20
Floyd Patterson becomes first former heavyweight champion to regain title, knocking out Ingemar Johansson in fifth round at Polo Grounds.

AUG. 2
Continental League folds following agreement that existing major leagues will expand for first time in 59 years. American and National Leagues will each add two teams no later than 1962.

SEPT. 11
Summer Olympics end in Rome with U.S. strong in track and swimming and Soviet Union winning most medals. American winners include boxer Cassius Clay, sprinter Wilma Rudolph, and men's basketball team.

OCT. 13
Pittsburgh Pirates win first World Series in 35 years when Bill Mazeroski homers in bottom of ninth inning of Game 7 to beat New York Yankees, 10–9.

NOV. 16
Early in Lakers' first season in Los Angeles, Elgin Baylor scores NBA-record 71 points against New York Knicks at Madison Square Garden.

DEC. 26
Philadelphia Eagles win first NFL championship in 11 years with 17–13 victory over Green Bay. Six days later, Houston Oilers beat Los Angeles Chargers, 24–16, in first AFL title game.

1961

JAN. 1
Sixth-ranked Washington beats No. 1 Minnesota, 17–7, in Rose Bowl, and No. 2 Mississippi defeats unranked Rice, 14–6, in Sugar Bowl.

MAR. 25
After two third-place Final Four finishes with Oscar Robertson, the University of Cincinnati finally wins NCAA title without the Big O. Bearcats beat Ohio State in overtime, 70–65.

APR. 16
Chicago Black Hawks win Stanley Cup for first time in 23 years, taking final series with Detroit in six games.

JULY 14
Arnold Palmer wins British Open by a stroke at Royal Birkdale, becoming first American winner since Ben Hogan in 1953.

OCT. 1
Roger Maris of the Yankees hits his 61st home run off Boston's Tracy Stallard to break Babe Ruth's single-season home run mark of 60 in 1927. Commissioner Ford Frick puts asterisk on new record because Maris played in eight more games than Ruth.

DEC. 6
Syracuse halfback Ernie Davis becomes first black player to win Heisman Trophy.

DEC. 31
Green Bay routs New York Giants, 37–0, to win NFL championship for first time since 1944.

1962

APR. 22
Toronto Maple Leafs beat defending champion Chicago in six games to win first Stanley Cup since 1951.

MAR. 2
Wilt Chamberlain of Philadelphia Warriors shatters NBA single-game scoring record with 100-point performance against New York Knicks in Hershey, Pa.

JUNE 29
Brazil scores twice in second half to beat Czechoslovakia, 3–1, in World Cup final at Santiago, Chile.

JUNE 17
Jack Nicklaus outshoots Arnold Palmer, 71–74, to win 18-hole playoff for U.S. Open championship. Victory marks first major for Nicklaus. Defeat comes between wins at Masters and British Open for Palmer.

SEPT. 11
Rod Laver wins U.S. singles title at Forest Hills, becoming second male player to win tennis Grand Slam in one year. He will turn pro in 1963.

SEPT. 25
Challenger Sonny Liston knocks out heavyweight champion Floyd Patterson at 2:06 of first round at Comiskey Park in Chicago.

OCT. 16
Ralph Terry, who gave up Bill Mazeroski's homer in relief to lose 1960 World Series, redeems himself by pitching 1–0 shutout over Giants in Game 7 of World Series.

NOVEMBER
NBA season opens with Wilt Chamberlain and Warriors transplanted from Philadelphia to San Francisco.

DEC. 23
Tommy Brooker's field goal at 2:54 of second overtime period lifts Dallas Texans to 20–17 victory over Houston in AFL title game. Texans will move to Kansas City and become Chiefs in 1963.

1963

JAN. 1
Top-ranked Southern Cal holds on to beat No. 2 Wisconsin, 42–37, in Rose Bowl. USC led, 42–14, after three quarters.

MAR. 23
Loyola of Chicago denies Cincinnati a third straight NCAA basketball title by upsetting the Bearcats in overtime, 60–58, in Louisville.

Wilt Chamberlain scores 100 points vs. Knicks, March 2, 1962.

Whatever shortcomings Rozelle

may have had as a GM, he was a savvy public relations man and proved to be a marketing genius as league czar. By the end of the sixties, he had defused a possible gambling scandal by suspending all-pros Paul Hornung and Alex Karras in 1963 for betting on their own teams to win, successfully countered a challenge by the rival American Football League, absorbed all 10 AFL clubs in a merger, and negotiated TV contracts that soared to $46.25 million a year in 1970 while insisting that all revenues be divided equally. ☙ **A 1960 Gallup poll** that asked Americans to name their favorite sport showed that 34 percent of the country was partial to baseball and 21 percent liked football. By the end of the decade the same poll revealed almost exactly the opposite. What happened? Football caught the imagination of the sixties and baseball didn't. From the "The Greatest Game Ever Played," between the Baltimore Colts and the New York Giants in the 1958 NFL Championship Game, to Joe Namath's "guaranteed" upset by the New York Jets over the Colts in the 1969 Super Bowl, pro football did nothing but get more popular. And the turnaround was orchestrated by Rozelle. Lamar Hunt—who founded the AFL in 1959, fought Rozelle for seven years, and helped broker a peace treaty between the warring leagues in 1966—would later call his old foe "the most important person in the history of professional football." ☙ **Hunt, the youngest son** of billionaire oilman H.L. Hunt, was one of the most important persons in the history of three professional sports in the sixties— football, soccer, and tennis. Early in 1960, when Rozelle tried to kill off the AFL by offering expansion teams to Hunt in Dallas, Bud Adams in Houston, and Max Winter in Minneapolis, Winter jumped but Hunt and Adams stayed put and saved the league. In

1969 when the North American Soccer League that Hunt helped establish teetered on the edge of extinction, he convinced former player and coach Phil Woosnam to run the league on a shoestring, and the NASL was able to stay afloat long enough to see the arrival of Brazilian World Cup hero Pele in 1975. ✍ **The long-running hypocrisy** of "shamateur" tennis gave way to Open Tennis in 1967 when All-England Club chairman Herman David declared that Wimbledon would allow professionals to compete in 1968. The year before, World Championship Tennis, an eight-man pro tour starring John Newcombe and Tony Roche, and the National Tennis League, which featured Rod Laver and Ken Rosewall, had signed up most of the world's best men's players. Hunt bankrolled the more efficiently run WCT and took on the NTL roster of players in 1970. ✍ **Laver won the Grand Slam** as an amateur in 1962, then did it again as a pro in 1969. The following year he won an unheard of $201,453 in prize money, $44,000 more than Lee Trevino, the top golfer on the PGA Tour. But tennis wasn't golf because tennis didn't have an Arnold Palmer. ✍ **Palmer never won golf's Grand Slam,** but he redefined it. Until he charged from behind to win both the Masters and U.S. Open in 1960, the Slam had always been the four titles Bobby Jones swept in 1930— the open and amateur championships of the United States and Britain. When Palmer decided to chase Ben Hogan's 1953 triple and play the British Open for the first time, golf writers added the PGA Championship to the mix and called it the "new" Grand Slam. Arnie finished second at St. Andrews and seventh at the PGA, but he had already established himself as the most charismatic athlete in America. ✍ **Palmer was golf's first** television star, the first player

APR. 17
NFL commissioner Pete Rozelle suspends Paul Hornung of Green Bay and Alex Karras of Detroit one year apiece for betting on their own teams to win.

JUNE 21
Florida A&M track star Bob Hayes sets new world record of 9.1 seconds in 100-yard dash.

JULY 22
Heavyweight champion Sonny Liston knocks out challenger Floyd Patterson in the first round again. This time the bell tolls at 2:10.

NOV. 10
Gordie Howe becomes NHL's all-time leading regular-season goal scorer, moving past Maurice Richard with No. 545.

DEC. 29
Chicago Bears win first NFL championship since 1946, beating New York Giants, 14–10, at Wrigley Field.

1964

JAN. 1
Top-ranked Texas sinks No. 2 Navy and Heisman Trophy-winning quarterback Roger Staubach, 28–6, in Cotton Bowl.

FEB. 9
Winter Olympics end in Innsbruck, Austria. Soviet Union dominates standings as speed skater Lydia Skoblikova wins four events.

MAR. 21
UCLA wins first NCAA basketball championship, beating Duke 98–83.

FEB. 25
Challenger Cassius Clay, a 7–1 underdog, wins heavyweight title when champion Sonny Liston refuses to answer bell to start seventh round. Liston said his left shoulder and arm were numb.

APR. 26
Boston Celtics become first team in professional sports to win six consecutive titles, beating San Francisco Warriors in five-game NBA final.

MAY 30
A.J. Foyt wins second Indianapolis 500, but race is marred by second-lap crash that kills racers Eddie Sachs and Dave McDonald.

JUNE 20
Ken Venturi overcomes heat prostration on final day of U.S. Open to card rounds of 66–70 and win his first tournament in four years and only major of his career.

OCTOBER
Tokyo Summer Olympics are dominated by U.S. and Soviet Union who win 186 medals between them. American swimmer Don Schollander leads all athletes with four gold medals.

OCT. 15
Bob Gibson hurls three complete games and wins twice to lead Cardinals over New York Yankees in seven-game World Series. Title is Cards' first since 1946.

NOV. 7
Eleven years after moving from Boston to Milwaukee, the Braves announce they'll be calling Atlanta home in 1965.

OCT. 25
Minnesota Vikings defensive end Jim Marshall picks up San Francisco fumble and runs 60 yards into his own end zone. Wrong-way "touchdown" is ruled a safety and 49ers are awarded two points.

1965

JAN. 13
San Francisco Warriors trade Wilt Chamberlain to Philadelphia 76ers for $150,000 and three players.

APR. 4
Sam Snead wins Greater Greensboro Open, becoming oldest PGA Tour winner at age 52. His 81st career victory is also an all-time high.

APR. 9
Astrodome opens in Houston as hometown Astros (formerly Colt .45s) beat New York Yankees, 2–1, in exhibition game.

APR. 15
Boston wins Game 7 of classic NBA Eastern Division finals against Philadelphia when John Havlicek steals an inbounds pass in last seconds. Celtics then beat Lakers in five-game NBA finals.

MAY 25
Heavyweight champion Muhammad Ali, who changed his name from Cassisus Clay in 1964, wins rematch with Sonny Liston on controversial first-round knockout in Lewiston, Maine.

JUNE 25
NHL announces that it will double its size with six expansion teams for 1966–67 season.

SEPT. 29
Dodgers southpaw Sandy Koufax becomes first pitcher in major league history to throw four no-hitters when he hurls 1–0 perfect game at Chicago Cubs in Los Angeles.

OCT. 14
Sandy Koufax throws his second shutout in three days to lead Los Angeles to a 2–0 victory over Minnesota in Game 7 of the World Series.

1966

JAN. 1
Fourth-ranked Alabama is able to win second straight national championship when top three schools—Michigan State, Arkansas, and Nebraska—all lose and final AP media poll is taken *after* bowl games for the first time.

MAR. 5
Major League Baseball Players Association elects Marvin Miller as executive director.

MAR. 19
Texas Western becomes the first team with an all-black starting five to win NCAA basketball title. The Miners beat all-white and top-ranked Kentucky, 72–65.

APR. 28
Boston Celtics win eighth straight NBA championship for retiring coach Red Auerbach. Lakers fall in seven games.

JUNE 8
AFL and NFL announce agreement to merge by 1970 season and stage world championship game between the champions of both leagues in January 1967.

JULY 9
Jack Nicklaus wins British Open at Muirfield, Scotland, joining Gene Sarazen, Ben Hogan, and Gary Player as only golfers to win all four majors.

JULY 17
University of Kansas freshman Jim Ryun breaks world mile record with time of 3:51.5.

Arnold Palmer flings visor after winning 1960 U.S. Open.

Arnie's Army

to have his own army of fans, the first to win the Masters four times, the first to earn $100,000 in prize money in one year, and the first to hire sports marketing mastermind Mark McCormack to manage his career. McCormack, who signed Palmer up in 1959 and started International Management Group a year later, turned Arnie into the first athlete–pitchman–conglomerate. *Sports Illustrated* writer E.M. Swift summed up McCormack's influence on the marriage of sports and commerce this way in a 1990 profile: "McCormack convinced the business world that sports was an ideal marketing vehicle— high in visibility, positive in image, and international in scope." **That was pretty much what** Roone Arledge had in mind when he developed the decade's ideal television vehicle, *Wide World of Sports*, the groundbreaking anthology series that ABC-TV first broadcast on April 29, 1961. Host and commentator Jim McKay promised a lot— "Spanning the globe to bring you the constant variety of sport: the thrill of victory and the agony of defeat, the human drama of athletic competition"—but *Wide World* delivered. **Originally hired in 1960** to produce NCAA football games for ABC's fledgling sports department, Arledge was also turned loose on *Wide World* and elevated it from a Saturday afternoon summer fill-in to the signature program of ABC Sports. By the seventies, Arledge's productions of the Olympic Games and the NFL's *Monday Night Football* were the signature programs of the whole network. ❧ **While television transformed sports** in the sixties, Arledge transformed the way TV covered sports, inventing as he went along and giving the viewer a better seat than someone at the game. He put long-range cameras in blimps and hand-held cameras on the sidelines. He perfected the use of slow-motion instant replays, isolated cameras, and field microphones. He employed close-ups and crowd shots and introduced story lines to dramatize every event. ❧ **One event Arledge** never had trouble dramatizing on *Wide World* was a Muhammad Ali fight. Bill Russell may have led the Boston Celtics to nine NBA championships in the decade, but Ali was the champion of the sixties. As Cassius Clay he won a gold medal at the 1960 Rome Olympics, turned pro that fall, and charmed the country by not only winning his first 19 fights, but by predicting the round in which many of his opponents would fall. He was a loudmouth and a tireless self-promoter, two qualities he elevated to an art form after doing a radio program with Gorgeous George in 1961 and being impressed with the antics of the aging but still outrageous pro wrestler. "When you're as great as I am," Clay crowed, "it's hard to be humble." Americans lapped it up, remembering what Dizzy Dean once said: "It ain't braggin' if you go out and do it." ❧ **Clay, a 7-to-1 underdog,** went out and did it to heavyweight champion Sonny Liston on February 25, 1964 ("Make a date, I'll get Sonny in eight!"). It only took seven. A month past his 22nd birthday, Clay had, in his words, "shook up the world." ❧ **Shortly after the fight** he shook the world again by announcing that he had joined the Black Muslim religious sect and had

JULY 30
England gets three goals from Geoff Hurst, two in overtime, to beat West Germany, 4–2, in World Cup final. A crowd of 93,802 sees game at London's Wembley Stadium.

1967

FEB. 2
American Basketball Association announces it will challenge NBA starting in fall.

APR. 11
Philadelphia wins NBA title after record 68-win regular season and five-game conquest of Boston in Eastern Division finals.

MAY 2
Toronto beats Montreal, four games to two, with oldest team ever to play in Stanley Cup finals. It will be last time Maple Leafs reach final round this century.

AUG. 20
Charlie Sifford becomes first black golfer to win PGA Tour event when he shoots final-round 64 to win Greater Hartford Open.

SEPT. 10
Billie Jean King and John Newcombe, who both won singles titles at Wimbledon in July, do the same at Forest Hills in the last year of the amateur era.

OCT. 18
AL approves of Kansas City A's move to Oakland in 1968 while adding expansion teams in Kansas City and Seattle. The NL will expand to San Diego and Montreal.

DEC. 14
British tennis officials vote for open tennis and admitting professionals to Wimbledon.

NOV. 19
Top-ranked Notre Dame and No. 2 Michigan State play to 10–10 tie in East Lansing. Both teams end season at 9–0–1. Final AP media poll names Irish national champions.

JAN. 15
First AFL-NFL World Championship Game ends with Green Bay defeating Kansas City, 35–10. A crowd of 61,946 sees game at L.A. Coliseum.

FEB. 6
Muhammad Ali unifies world heavyweight title by outpointing WBA champion Ernie Terrell in 15 rounds at Astrodome.

APR. 28
Muhammad Ali is stripped of his heavyweight title by the WBA and most state boxing commissions after refusing induction into U.S. Army because of his Black Muslin religion.

MAY 31
A.J. Foyt wins third Indianapolis 500 in seven years. In June, he and Dan Gurney go to France to win 24 Hours of Le Mans.

OCT. 1
Boston wins wild four-way pennant race in AL, beating out Minnesota and Detroit by one game and Chicago by three. Flag is first for Red Sox since 1946.

OCT. 12
"Impossible dream" ends for Red Sox as St. Louis beats Boston, 7–2, in Game 7 of World Series.

NOV. 18
O.J. Simpson's 64-yard touchdown run in the fourth quarter enables Southern Cal to beat top-ranked UCLA, 21–20, and win Rose Bowl berth. Victory also gives USC national championship in final AP media poll.

1968

JAN. 14
Green Bay wins second AFL-NFL World Championship Game with 33–14 victory over Oakland at Orange Bowl in Miami.

JAN. 20
Elvin Hayes and University of Houston upset Lew Alcindor and UCLA, 71–69, at Astrodome in Houston. Defeat snaps UCLA's 47-game winning streak.

FEBRUARY
Winter Olympics at Grenoble, France, feature Jean-Claude Killy winning all three men's alpine skiing events and America's Peggy Fleming taking the gold medal in women's figure skating.

MAR. 22–23
UCLA thrashes top-ranked Houston, 101–69, in NCAA semifinals then routs North Carolina by 23 points in championship game.

MAR. 30
International Lawn Tennis Federation endorses open tennis. Professionals and amateurs will be allowed to play together as in golf.

APR. 14
Bob Goalby and Roberto De Vicenzo tie for Masters lead at 277 after four rounds. Goalby declared winner, however, when De Vicenzo signs incorrect scorecard.

SEPT. 9
Arthur Ashe becomes first black male to win national singles title, as Forest Hills hosts initial U.S. Open.

SEPT. 14
Detroit pitcher Denny McLain becomes baseball's first 30-game winner since Dizzy Dean in 1934. Tigers beat Oakland, 5–4.

OCTOBER
Americans dominate Mexico City Summer Olympics which are noted for Bob Beamon's world record long jump and the black power salutes of Tommie Smith and John Carlos.

1969

JAN. 1
Top-ranked Ohio State beats No. 2 Southern Cal, 27–16, in Rose Bowl to clinch 1968 national championship.

JAN. 12
New York Jets upset 19-point favorite Baltimore Colts, 16–7, in Super Bowl III at Orange Bowl in Miami.

MAR. 22
Lew Alcindor era ends at UCLA as Bruins beat Purdue, 92–72, for third straight NCAA title.

MAY 5
Celtics beat Lakers, 108–106, in Game 7 of NBA finals to win ninth title of decade and 11th in 13 years. Player-coach Bill Russell will retire as both in July.

JUNE 24–25
Longest match in Wimbledon history ends with 41-year-old Pancho Gonzales beating Charlie Pasarell 22–24, 1–6, 16–14, 6–3, 11–9 in five hours and 12 minutes.

SEPT. 8
Seven years after winning tennis Grand Slam as an amateur, Rod Laver wins U.S. Open at Forest Hills to duplicate feat as a pro.

OCT. 16
New York Mets upset Baltimore to win World Series in five games.

DEC. 5
Top-ranked Texas rallies from 14–0 deficit in fourth quarter to beat No. 2 Arkansas, 15–14, and secure national title.

Four-time Olympic discus champion Al Oerter uncoils in 1968.

changed his name to Muhammad Ali. In a divisive decade marked by political assassination, civil rights demonstrations, and an unpopular war in Vietnam, Ali became a national lightning rod. When he refused induction into the military on religious grounds in 1967, he was immediately stripped of the title he had defended nine times and within two months he was found guilty of draft evasion and sentenced to five years in jail. ❧ **Barred from the ring** but free on appeal, Ali waited 41 months before the U.S. Supreme Court reversed his conviction in 1971. During that time the country came around to his thinking on the war. ❧ **The year after Ali's conviction,** Tommie Smith set a world record in the 200-meter race at the 1968 Summer Olympics in Mexico City and teammate John Carlos finished third. Their protest of racism in America by raising their fists on the winners' platform during the playing of the national anthem was the most visible display of the decade's Black Power movement in sports. ❧

Smith and Carlos

Arthur Ashe, who became the first black man to win a major championship in tennis when he won the U.S. Open in 1968, felt that Ali's refusal to be inducted had a great influence on the movement. "He was largely responsible for it becoming an expected part of a black athlete's responsibility to get involved," said Ashe. "He had more at stake than any of us." ❧

The U.S. won its first gold medal in Olympic hockey in 1960, sweeping Canada, the Soviet Union, and Czechoslovakia in the final three games. At right, American defenseman Weldy Olson chases Czech forward Miroslav Vlach. Below, coach Jack Riley (the feet without skates) dives into celebration after his boys upset Canada, 2–1.

Figure skater Peggy Fleming was 19 when she won the only U.S. gold medal at the 1968 Winter Olympics in Grenoble, France. She went on to popularize the sport in ice shows and on television as a commentator.

The most outstanding athletic achievement of the decade was Bob Beamon's gold-medal-winning leap at the 1968 Summer Olympics in Mexico City. He didn't just set a new world record of 29 feet, 2$\frac{1}{2}$ inches, he obliterated the old mark by nearly two feet. The record would stand for 23 years.

American sprinter Wilma Rudolph (below), who wore a brace on her left leg as a child, ran off with three gold medals in 1960. Eight years later in Mexico City, Dick Fosbury's innovative "flop" not only won the high jump, it revolutionized the event.

Bob Hayes lived up to his title, "world's fastest human," at the 1964 Tokyo Olympics. Seen here coasting to victory in a preliminary heat, he won the 100-meter final by equaling the world record of 10.0 seconds. He followed that up in the 4 x 100 relay by running an astonishing 8.9-second anchor leg for a come-from-behind victory.

Green Bay linemen Forrest Gregg (left) and Jerry Kramer (64) carry an exultant coach Vince Lombardi off the field after the Packers beat Oakland, 33–14, to win their second straight AFL–NFL World Championship Game, on January 14, 1968. Three weeks later Lombardi stepped down as head coach.

T he cruel side of pro football. Above, Philadelphia's Chuck Bednarik celebrates after a hit on Frank Gifford, which knocked the Giants' halfback out not only for the moment but for more than a season. Right, Giants quarterback Y.A. Tittle, battered and beaten by the Pittsburgh Steelers late in his career.

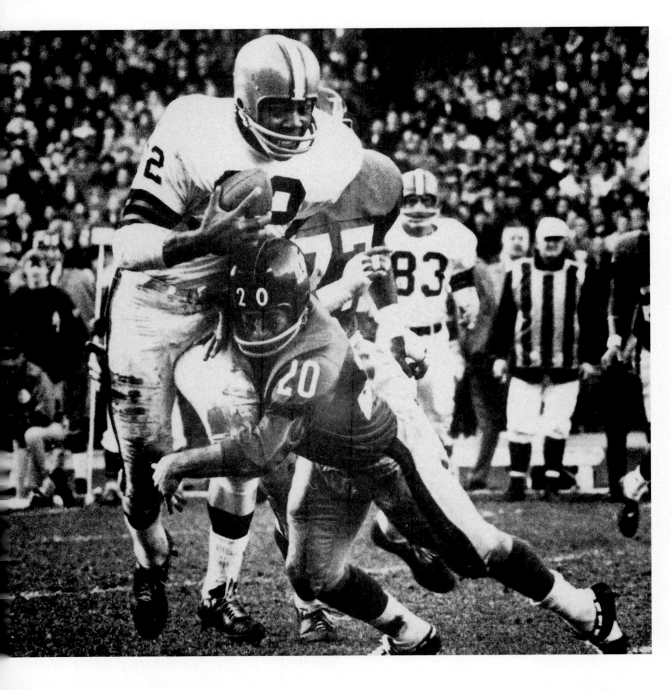

From 1957 to 1965 the toughest thing to do in the NFL was tackle Cleveland fullback Jim Brown. In his nine years as a pro, Brown led the league in rushing eight times, averaged 5.2 yards a carry, and never missed a down due to injury.

It's one thing to guarantee victory when you are a 19-point underdog. It's another to pull it off. Quarterback Joe Namath and the New York Jets did both against the Baltimore Colts in Super Bowl III.

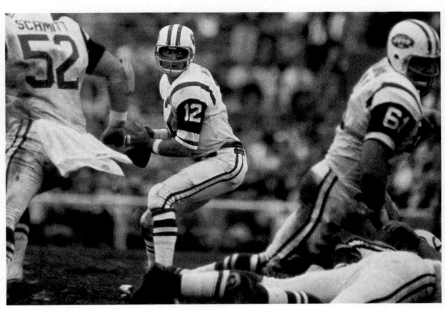

In three consecutive Junes, young Jack Nicklaus finished second to Arnold Palmer as an amateur in the 1960 U.S. Open, won the 1961 NCAA championship as a senior at Ohio State, then beat Palmer in a playoff to claim the 1962 U.S. Open as a rookie on the PGA Tour.

Australia's Rod Laver won the Grand Slam twice in the sixties, once as an amateur in 1962 and again as a professional in 1969. Here he is engaged in a four-set victory over countryman John Newcombe at Wimbledon in 1969. The advent of Open Tennis in 1968 allowed pros to compete for major national championships previously contested by amateurs only.

Toronto forward Frank Mahovlich, upended here by Detroit defenseman Bill Gadsby, led the Maple Leafs to their third straight Stanley Cup title in 1964. Despite the NHL's doubling in size in the sixties, the two Canadian teams—Toronto and Montreal—won nine of 10 Stanley Cups.

Although being forcibly evicted from his seat in this picture, Larry Mahan was the All-Around Cowboy Champion at the National Finals Rodeo for five consecutive years, from 1966 to 1970.

Geoff Hurst scores the winner in the 1966 World Cup final against Germany. Hurst scored England's first goal, and then, in overtime, completed the only hat trick ever in a World Cup final.

In three seasons at Louisiana State ending with his senior year in 1969–70, Pete Maravich averaged 44.2 points per game—and that was 17 years before the NCAA introduced the three-point basket. Unfortunately, Pistol Pete never performed on a national stage because none of his LSU teams ever qualified for the NCAA tournament.

From 1962 to 1966, Sandy Koufax threw three no-hitters and one perfect game (left), led the Dodgers to two World Series titles, and dominated the major leagues in strikeouts, ERA, and wins.

The only time a World Series has been won on a home run in the bottom of the ninth inning of the ultimate game came on October 13, 1960. That's when Pittsburgh's Bill Mazeroski knocked a shot over the left field wall, breaking a 9–9 tie with the Yankees. As Maz circled the bases (far left), eyewitnesses rejoiced from sold-out Forbes Field to the observation deck at the nearby Cathedral of Learning on the campus of the University of Pittsburgh.

Bobby Orr, after scoring overtime goal to win 1970 Stanley Cup

1970–1979

In 1971, the fourth year

of Open Tennis, Stan Smith and Billie Jean King won the singles championships at the U.S. Open. Smith was handed a winner's check for $15,000 and King got $7,500. A year later, King and Ilie Nastase were the toast of Forest Hills, only this time Nastase's $25,000 in prize money was two and half times the $10,000 King received. ✒ **Angry that the gap** between winners' purses was widening rather than closing, King told tournament officials, "If it isn't equal next year, I won't play, and I don't think the other women will either." The next summer, the U.S. Open became the first grand slam tournament to offer the same prize money to men and women. King's threat and the result she obtained put her in the forefront of the national women's movement and revolutionized women's rights in sports during the boom years of the seventies. ✒ **When promoters insisted** on giving men preferential treatment in the early days of Open Tennis, King led a 1970 walkout that resulted in a separate women's tour run by *World Tennis* magazine publisher Gladys Heldman and sponsored by Virginia Slims, a new Philip Morris cigarette for women that carried the catch phrase, "You've Come A Long Way, Baby." By the end of the decade, annual prize money

Billie Jean King

1970

JAN. 1
No. 1 Texas rallies in closing seconds to defeat No. 9 Notre Dame, 21–17, in Cotton Bowl. First bowl for Irish in 45 years.

JAN.11
Underdog Kansas City Chiefs give AFL second straight Super Bowl victory over NFL. Minnesota beaten, 23–7, in New Orleans.

FEB. 16
Joe Frazier stops Jimmy Ellis in fifth round to win heavyweight championship involuntarily vacated by Muhammad Ali in 1967.

MARCH
Pete Maravich of LSU ends collegiate basketball career with all-time record scoring average of 44.2 over three seasons. Never makes it to NCAA tournament, however.

MAY 8
New York Knicks win their first NBA championship, beating Los Angeles, 113–99, in Game 7 at Madison Square Garden.

MAY 10
Boston Bruins sweep St. Louis to capture their first Stanley Cup since 1941. Bobby Orr scores clinching goal in overtime of Game 4.

JUNE 21
Brazil routs Italy, 4–1, in Mexico City to win third World Cup in last four tournaments.

JUNE 21
Tony Jacklin becomes first English golfer to win U.S. Open since Ted Ray in 1920.

SEPT. 13
Margaret Smith Court becomes second woman to win calendar-year Grand Slam with victory in U.S. Open.

SEPT. 21
ABC-TV airs first Monday Night Football game. Browns down New York Jets, 31–21, in Cleveland.

OCT. 15
Baltimore Orioles return to World Series, whip Cincinnati in five games in first Series played on artificial turf.

OCT. 26
Former heavyweight champion Muhammad Ali returns from exile after 3½ years, stopping Gerry Quarry in third round at Atlanta.

1971

JAN. 1
Third-ranked Nebraska wins first national title when No. 1 Texas and No. 2 Ohio State lose bowl games. Cornhuskers beat LSU in Orange Bowl.

JAN. 17
In Super Bowl V, Baltimore beats Dallas, 16–13, on last-second 32-yard field goal by Jim O'Brien.

APRIL
Boston's Phil Esposito (76 goals) and Bobby Orr (102 assists) set single-season scoring records, but Bruins are dethroned as Stanley Cup champions by Montreal.

MAR. 8
Joe Frazier scores unanimous 15-round decision over Muhammad Ali at Madison Square Garden in first-ever meeting of undefeated heavyweight champions. Fight grosses $23 million as 300 million watch via satellite and closed circuit TV.

APRIL 8
First legal off-track betting parlor in U.S. opens in New York City.

APR. 30
Milwaukee Bucks, led by Lew Alcindor and Oscar Robertson, sweep Baltimore Bullets in NBA finals.

JUNE 28
U.S. Supreme Court votes 8–0 to overturn Muhammad Ali's 1967 conviction for draft evasion.

OCT. 3
Billie Jean King wins Phoenix stop on Virginia Slims tour, becoming first sportswoman to earn $100,000 in one year.

NOV. 25
Top-ranked Nebraska (10–0) rallies to beat No. 2 Oklahoma (9–0) by 35–31 score on Thanksgiving.

1972

JAN. 8
NCAA announces freshman will be eligible to play football and basketball at major universities beginning in the fall.

FEB. 20
Three-time Indianapolis 500 winner A.J. Foyt wins Daytona 500 with record average speed of 161.550 mph.

MAR. 19
Immaculata College wins first Association for Intercollegiate Athletics for Women national basketball tournament.

APR. 13
First general players' strike in baseball history ends after one week. Pension dispute settled, season abbreviated by 86 games.

MAY 7
After losing seven out of 10 NBA finals since 1962, the Los Angeles Lakers finally win title, beating New York four games to one.

JUNE 19
U.S. Supreme Court votes 5–3 to uphold baseball's exemption from antitrust laws. Decision ends Curt Flood suit challenging reserve clause.

JUNE 23
President Richard Nixon signs Higher Education Act of 1972 (Title IX) into law, prohibiting sex bias in athletic programs at colleges receiving federal assistance.

JUNE 27
Chicago Black Hawks star Bobby Hull signs $2.75 million contract to play for Winnipeg Jets of new World Hockey Association starting in fall.

SEPTEMBER
Team Canada wins last three games of landmark eight-game "Summit Series" with Soviet Union. NHL claims victory with four wins, three losses, and a tie.

SEPT. 5–6
Munich Summer Olympics held hostage when Arab terrorists kill two members of Israeli team and kidnap nine others. Airport gun battle claims 15 more lives. Tragedy comes day after U.S. swimmer Mark Spitz wins last of his record seven gold medals.

OCT. 13–15
Stan Smith leads U.S. to 3–2 victory over Ilie Nastase and Romania in raucous Davis Cup final at Bucharest.

DEC. 23
"Immaculate Reception" by Pittsburgh's Franco Harris gives Steelers 13–7 victory over Oakland in AFC playoffs.

Bears middle linebacker Dick Butkus stops Packers.

on the Virginia Slims Tour leapt from $250,000 to $6.2 million. ❧ In 1971, King became the first woman athlete to earn $100,000 in prize money in any sport. A year later Congress passed Title IX, the Civil Rights Act amendment that mandated equal treatment for women by educational institutions, particularly in the participation and funding of athletics. And then in 1973, King took on self-proclaimed male chauvinist Bobby Riggs in a $100,000 winner-take-all "Battle of the Sexes" at the Astrodome that was one of the most anticipated sports events of the decade. The 55-year-old Riggs, who had beaten Margaret Smith Court, the women's number-one player, earlier in the year, was favored over the second-ranked King. But with a TV audience of over 50 million looking on, King routed Riggs in three straight sets and lifted the spirits of women worldwide. ❧ Meanwhile, another revolutionary was at work lifting the spirits and salaries of Major League Baseball players. Marvin Miller, a tough steel-industry labor leader who had become executive director of the players' union in 1966, immediately set about shifting the balance of power in baseball from the owners to the players. After extracting two basic agreements from the owners in 1967 and 1969, Miller beat them again when they dared the players to strike over pension benefits at the start of the 1972 season. The players went out, held their ground, and the first mass strike in the history of professional sports ended when the owners' resolve weakened and they gave in after 13 days. ❧ Later that year, the U.S. Supreme Court voted down former St. Louis Cardinals outfielder Curt Flood's

Curt Flood

suit challenging the reserve clause that bound a player to his club for life. Miller decided to go after the reserve clause at the bargaining table and in 1973 secured an agreement with owners to accept impartial binding arbitration of salary disputes. A year later, Oakland A's pitcher Catfish Hunter became a free agent when arbitrator Peter Seitz ruled that A's owner Charlie Finley had not lived up to his part of Hunter's $100,000-a-year contract. Less than three weeks later, the Yankees signed Hunter to a three-year, $3.75 million deal. ❧ **Miller then found a loophole** in the reserve clause, which said once a player's contract expired the club had the right to renew it for one year on the same terms. Owners had always interpreted that to mean they could keep renewing the contract year after year for as long as they wanted. Miller thought one year meant just that, one year. In 1975, pitchers Andy Messersmith of the Dodgers and Dave McNally of the Expos agreed to test his theory by refusing to sign contracts and then declaring themselves free agents at the end of the season. ❧ **When the case went before** a three-man arbitration board that included Miller, Seitz, and owners' representative John Gaherin, it was up to Seitz to cast the deciding vote. He sided with the players after pleading with the owners to settle. "They were too stupid and stubborn," Seitz said later. "They had accumulated so much power they wouldn't share it with anybody." Claiming the ruling would bankrupt baseball, the owners tried to have it overturned in the U.S. Court of Appeals, but failed. The reserve clause was dead. ❧ **In 1973, only five percent** of the players in Major League Baseball made $100,000 or more. By 1979 the average salary was $121,000. Over the same period, the designated hitter was introduced in the American League, Hank Aaron broke Babe

1973

JAN. 11
American League adopts designated hitter rule on three-year trial basis.

JAN. 14
Miami Dolphins complete first undefeated season (17–0) in NFL history with 14–7 victory over Washington in Super Bowl VII.

JAN. 22
Challenger George Foreman knocks down heavyweight champion Joe Frazier six times on way to second-round TKO in Kingston, Jamaica.

MARCH 26
Bill Walton scores record 44 points in NCAA title game to lead UCLA to its seventh consecutive championship and ninth in 10 years.

JUNE 9
Secretariat wins Belmont by astonishing 31 lengths to become first Triple Crown winner in 25 years.

SEPT. 17
Billie Jean King, 29, beats Bobby Riggs, 55, in straight sets to win "Battle of Sexes" before 30,492 at Astrodome and millions more watching on worldwide television.

DEC. 16
Buffalo's O.J. Simpson finishes NFL regular season with record 2,003 yards rushing in 332 attempts. Jim Brown set old record of 1,863 on 291 carries in 1963.

DEC. 31
Third-ranked Notre Dame wrests national championship from No. 1 Alabama by winning Sugar Bowl, 24–23. Game features six lead changes.

1974

FEB. 17
NASCAR officials shorten Daytona 500 to 450 miles due to national energy crisis. Richard Petty wins race for fifth time.

JAN. 19
Notre Dame basketball team rallies from 11 points down with 3:32 to play to snap UCLA's three-year, 88-game winning streak. Irish win, 71–70, in South Bend.

APR. 8
Hank Aaron slugs 715th career home run off Dodgers' Al Downing to pass Babe Ruth as baseball's all-time home run leader.

MAR. 23
Top-seeded North Carolina State meets No. 2 UCLA in NCAA tournament semifinal. Wolfpack wins, 80–77, in double overtime, then beats Marquette by 12 in final.

APR. 25
NFL owners vote to move goalposts to rear of end zone and allow 15-minute sudden-death overtime period to break ties during regular season.

MAY 19
Houston Aeroes win WHA championship, led by former NHL superstar Gordie Howe and his sons Mark and Marty. Howe, who came out of retirement at age 45, is also league MVP.

JUNE 12
Little League officials bow to social pressure, allow girls to play organized baseball.

JULY 7
Franz Beckenbauer and West Germany defeat Johan Cruyff and Holland, 2–1, in World Cup final at Munich.

AUG. 29
Utah Stars of ABA sign 19-year-old Moses Malone, making him first player to go directly to pros from high school.

OCT. 17
Oakland A's beat Los Angeles Dodgers in five games to become only team other than Yankees to win three consecutive World Series.

OCT. 30
Muhammad Ali reclaims heavyweight title with stunning eighth-round knockout of undefeated champion George Foreman in "Rumble in the Jungle" in Zaire.

DEC. 20
NFL player reserve system ruled illegal by federal judge, opening door to eventual free agency in pro football.

1975

JAN. 12
After 42 years of frustration, Pittsburgh owner Art Rooney finally wins NFL championship, as Steelers belt Minnesota, 16–7, in Super Bowl IX.

MAR. 31
UCLA gives John Wooden nicest going-away present a legendary coach could ask for: a 10th national title. Kentucky falls, 92–85.

JUNE 3
Brazilian legend Pele, 34, comes out of retirement to sign three-year, $7 million contract to play for New York Cosmos of North American Soccer League.

JULY 5
Arthur Ashe stuns heavily favored Jimmy Connors in four sets to become first black male to win Wimbledon singles title.

SEPT. 6
Chris Evert wins first of six U.S. Opens and ends season as world's No. 1 women's player for first time.

OCT. 1
Heavyweight champion Muhammad Ali meets archrival Joe Frazier a third time in classic "Thrilla in Manila." Ali wins when Frazier's corner throws in towel after 14th round.

OCT. 22
Cincinnati wins Game 7, but World Series image that endures is Carlton Fisk's 12th-inning homer off left field foul pole to win Game 6 for Red Sox.

DEC. 6
Ohio State running back Archie Griffin becomes only player to ever win Heisman Trophy twice.

DEC. 23
In major victory for baseball players' union, arbitrator Peter Seitz rules pitchers Andy Messersmith and Dave McNally are free agents after completing option year on their contracts.

1976

FEB. 5
Vermonter Bill Koch wins first Olympic medal ever by an American nordic skier at Winter Games in Innsbruck. Employing his revolutionary skating technique, he places second in 30-kilometer race.

MAR. 29
Unbeaten Hoosiers vanquish Michigan, 86–66, in NCAA championship game. Title first for Indiana since 1953.

Carlton Fisk reacts to Game 6 homer, 1975 World Series.

Ruth's career home run record, television audiences more than tripled when the World Series was moved to prime time, the Reds beat the Red Sox in a seven-game Series for the ages, and attendance soared from 30 million to 43.5 million customers a year. 🐦

The boom years of the seventies

came on the heels of the team sports expansion binge of the sixties. In 1959, the big leagues in America consisted of only 42 teams—16 in baseball, 12 in football, eight in basketball, and six in hockey. Fifteen years later, over 125 new teams, nine leagues and two new sports—soccer and tennis—had been added to the mix in the mad scramble to cash in on the country's mania for spectator sports. By the eighties, half of those new teams were gone. One of the new leagues, the American Football League, had managed to survive intact before merging with its rival. 🐦

Another league that survived the

decade was the North American Soccer League, whose New York Cosmos lured the world's greatest player, 34-year-old Pele of Brazil, out of retirement in 1975 with a three-year contract worth $7 million. Pele, who had quit as a player in 1970 after leading Brazil to three World Cup titles in four tournaments, gave the NASL its first name player, and he filled stadiums everywhere the Cosmos played. 🐦 **One league that didn't make it** to the eighties was the World Hockey Association, which went out of business in 1979, but allowed the NHL's all-time leading scorer, Gordie Howe, to leave retirement at age 45 and play with sons Mark and Marty for the Houston Aeros. Howe didn't retire again until he was 52 and back in the NHL for one season with the New England Whalers. 🐦

Hockey showcased the decade's major

showdown of international superpowers when an all-star team of the best Canadian players in the

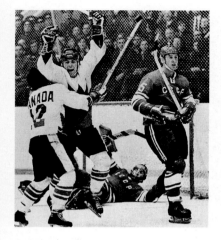

Henderson's deciding goal

NHL met the national team of the Soviet Union in September 1972. Heavily favored Team Canada won the dramatic and very competitive eight-game Summit Series, but just barely, needing a Paul Henderson goal in the final minute of the last game to take the series with a record of 4–3–1. ✪ Outside Canada, Muhammad Ali's return to boxing generated the most news of the seventies, especially his three exhausting fights (41 rounds) with Joe Frazier and his victory over George Foreman. Ali–Frazier I, which matched two undefeated world champions at Madison Square Garden on March 8, 1971, and paid them each two and half million dollars, was the most anticipated heavyweight title fight in history and ended with a decision in Frazier's favor after 15 rounds. Frazier lost the title two years later when 24-year-old George Foreman knocked him down six times in the first two rounds and the referee stopped the fight. ✪ Ali, now 32, met Foreman for the title in Zaire in 1974 and shocked the world one more time by winning the "Rope-a-Dope" fight with a knockout in the eighth round. He fought Frazier nine months before the Foreman fight and again 11 months after, winning both times, first by decision in New York and then by TKO in 14 rounds in the "Thrilla in Manila." ✪ The decade was full of irresistible forces, like Super Bowl TV ratings, the Steelers, UCLA basketball, Montreal hockey, Jack Nicklaus, Richard Petty, Bobby Orr, Mark Spitz, Secretariat, and Howard Cosell. But the immovable object—International Olympic Committee president Avery Brundage—finally gave way after 20 years, bowing

JUNE 6
Boston outlasts Phoenix, 128–126, in triple-overtime thriller to even NBA finals at 3–3. Celtics go on to win 13th title in 20 years.

JUNE 17
ABA decides to fold after nine seasons when NBA agrees to take in four franchises—Denver, Indiana, New Jersey, and San Antonio.

AUG. 1
Summer Olympics end in Montreal with star performances by 14-year-old Romanian gymnast Nadia Comaneci and the U.S. boxing team that features three future world champions (Leonard and the Spinks brothers).

OCT. 21
New York Yankees return to World Series for first time since 1964 and are swept by Cincinnati.

NOV. 4
Baseball holds first re-entry draft for 26 players who have played out their options.

1977

MAR. 28
Marquette sends coach Al McGuire into retirement with 67–59 victory over North Carolina in NCAA championship game.

JAN. 9
Oakland Raiders beat Minnesota, 32–14, in first Super Bowl played at Rose Bowl. Title game loss is Vikings' fourth in four appearances.

MAY 30
A.J. Foyt wins Indianapolis 500 for fourth time, but is upstaged by Janet Guthrie, the first woman to qualify for race.

JUNE 11
Seattle Slew becomes decade's second Triple Crown winner and history's 10th with four-length victory in Belmont.

JULY 2
Bjorn Borg beats Jimmy Connors in majestic five-setter as Wimbledon celebrates 100th anniversary. But Centre Court's most popular winner is England's Virginia Wade, who won women's title the day before.

JULY 9
Co-leaders after three rounds, Tom Watson outshoots Jack Nicklaus, 65–66, in memorable final round of British Open at Turnberry in Scotland.

SEPT. 13–18
Ted Turner skippers *Courageous* to four straight victories over challenger *Australia* in America's Cup.

OCT. 18
Reggie Jackson establishes reputation as "Mr. October" with three successive home runs in final game of Yankees' six-game World Series victory over Los Angeles.

1978

FEB. 15
Leon Spinks, a 24-year-old longshot with only seven pro fights to his credit, upsets 36-year-old heavyweight champion Muhammad Ali in 15-round split decision in Las Vegas.

MAR. 27
Top-seeded Kentucky wins NCAA basketball title for first time in 20 years, defeating Duke 94–88.

MAY 25
Led by Guy Lafleur and Ken Dryden, Montreal beats Boston in six-game final to win Stanley Cup for third year in a row and fifth time in decade.

JUNE 9
Unbeaten heavyweight Larry Holmes outslugs WBC champion Ken Norton in furious 15th round to win split decision and title in Las Vegas.

JUNE 18
A week after winning her first major LPGA Championship, 21-year-old rookie sensation Nancy Lopez wins record fifth straight tournament in Rochester, N.Y.

SEPT. 15
Muhammad Ali wins heavyweight title for record third time with lopsided 15-round decision over champion Leon Spinks in New Orleans. Judges' cards: 11–4, 10–4–1, 10–4–1.

OCT. 17
Fourteen games out of first place in mid-July, Yankees go on 52–21 tear to catch Boston, beat Red Sox in one-game playoff for division title, beat Kansas City for AL pennant, and beat Los Angeles in six-game World Series.

JUNE 7
Swept from NBA finals in both 1971 and '75, the Washington Bullets finally win championship with 105–99 victory in Game 7 against Seattle.

JUNE 10
Affirmed beats Alydar by a head to win Belmont Stakes and Triple Crown. Alydar is first horse to finish second in all three races.

JULY 7
Martina Navratilova beats Chris Evert in three sets to win her first Wimbledon singles title.

OCT. 8
Mario Andretti becomes first American since Phil Hill in 1961 to win Formula One driving championship.

1979

JAN. 1
Second-ranked Alabama beats No. 1 Penn State, 14–7, in Sugar Bowl to earn national title in final AP Top 20 poll.

MAR. 26
Magic Johnson and Michigan State beat Larry Bird and Indiana State, 75–64, in NCAA championship game.

SEPT. 9
Sixteen-year-old Tracy Austin becomes youngest player to win U.S. Open, beating Chris Evert Lloyd, 6–4, 6–3. Austin is 82 days younger than Maureen Connolly was in 1951.

OCT. 17
Down three games to one in World Series, Pittsburgh storms back to win three in a row against Baltimore.

JAN. 21
Pittsburgh Steelers become first team to win three Super Bowls, holding off two-time champion Dallas to win, 35–31.

JUNE 22
With WHA folding after seven seasons, NHL takes in four franchises: Edmonton, Hartford, Quebec, and Winnipeg.

SEPT. 16
In first Ryder Cup to add European golfers to Britain–Ireland side, American pros win, 17–11, at Greenbrier in West Virginia.

NOV. 30
Sugar Ray Leonard wins first world boxing title, stopping welterweight champion Wilfred Benitez in 15th round.

Police move to counter Munich terrorists, 1972.

out following the 1972 Summer Olympics in Munich where he insisted the games continue despite the murders of 11 Israeli athletes and coaches by Palestinian terrorists. ❧ **Brundage, the Chicago-born** millionaire idealist, held sway over domestic and international amateur sports for nearly half a century as president of the American Athletic Union (1928–35), president of the U.S. Olympic Committee (1929–53) and president of the IOC (1952–72). He was Jim Thorpe's teammate at the 1912 Stockholm Olympics and competed against him in the pentathlon and decathlon that year. But he did nothing to help the drive to reinstate Thorpe's forfeited gold medals the entire time he ran the IOC. For the so-called "apostle of amateurism," it was a non-issue. An amateur derives no income from sport, not even summer semi-pro baseball for $25 a game. The IOC eventually exonerated Thorpe in 1982. ❧ **Writer Allen Guttmann** summed up Brundage this way in his book *The Games Must Go On*: "He was usually seen by those Americans who were aware of him at all as a crusty octogenarian bureaucrat given to sour statements about amateurism and its corruption. A spoilsport. An anachronism." ❧ **His retirement cleared the way** for an Open Olympics, but it would take 20 more years before professionals were finally allowed to compete. ❧

Arthur Ashe winning Wimbledon, 1975

Soviet goaltender Vladislav Tretiak gathers in a shot by Canada's Frank Mahovlich (27) in Game 1 of the eight-game USSR–Canada summit series in 1972. The Soviets stunned the Canadian squad of NHL All-Stars with two wins and a tie in the first four games, played in Canada. The venue then changed to Moscow, where Team Canada lost Game 5, then rallied to win three in a row to clinch the series. Barely.

Pete Rose played in five World Series from 1970 to 1980, winning three times. Unlike Jackson, Rose's nickname of "Charlie Hustle" didn't apply to just the postseason. Rose hustled all the time. He also outhit every major leaguer who ever played, retiring in 1986 with more base hits (4,256) than any other player in history.

Mark Spitz won seven gold medals at the 1972 Munich Olympics and set world records in each event. His final medal, awarded for the butterfly leg of the 400-meter medley relay (right), came the day before Arab terrorists invaded the Olympic Village.

Before Romania's 14-year-old Nadia Comeneci came along in 1976, no Olympic gymnast had ever scored a perfect 10 in any event. By the end of the Montreal Games, Comeneci had earned seven 10s on the way to gold medals in the all-around, uneven bars, and balance beam.

Muhammad Ali was stripped of his heavyweight title in 1967 after refusing induction into the U.S. Army. He emerged from boxing exile in 1970 and fought Joe Frazier for the championship in 1971. Frazier (far right) won by unanimous decision after dropping Ali with this roundhouse left in the 15th round. Two years later, Frazier lost his crown to George Foreman, setting up the Ali–Foreman "Rumble in the Jungle" in Zaire (above). Ali won his title back, knocking Foreman out in the eighth round.

U CLA's streak of seven straight NCAA basketball titles was broken in the semifinals of the 1974 Final Four. David Thompson and North Carolina State edged the Bruins of Bill Walton and Keith Wilkes, 80–77, in double overtime. The 29–1 Wolfpack then beat Marquette by 12 points for their first championship.

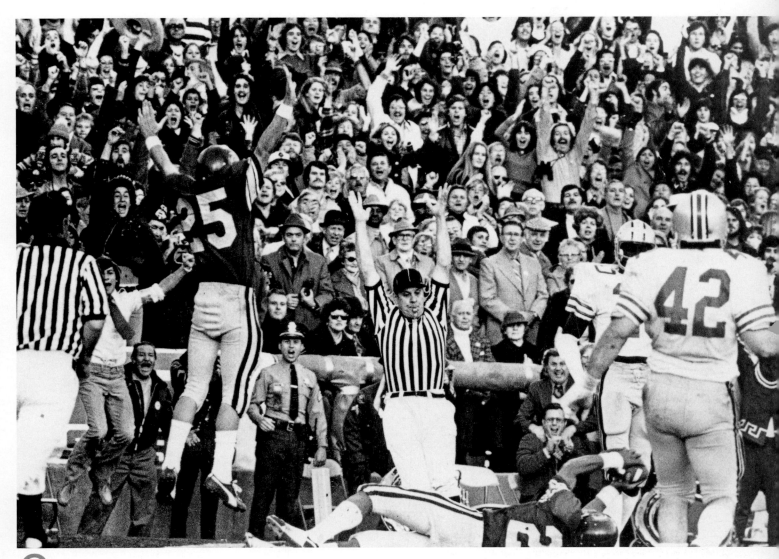

Ohio State led Southern California, 17–10, with two minutes remaining in the 1975 Rose Bowl. But Pat Haden completed a 38-yard touchdown pass in the final moments, then hit Shelton Diggs (holding ball) with a two-point pass to give the Trojans an 18–17 victory and the national championship.

Playing at home on December 26, 1977, the Los Angeles Rams thought they would finally play the Minnesota Vikings in good weather, but a major storm turned the Coliseum field into a quagmire. In a game since known as the "Mud Bowl," the Vikings clinched the victory when Sammy Johnson scored in the fourth quarter.

Affirmed and Alydar finished 1–2 in all three Triple Crown events of 1978.
After losing by a length and a half in the Kentucky Derby, and a neck in the Preakness,
Alydar closed the gap to a head in the Belmont but could get no closer.

As jockey Ron Turcotte glances back at the field of horses fading behind him, Secretariat runs off with a 31-length victory in the 1973 Belmont Stakes. The horse captured the first Triple Crown since Citation in 1948, but the racing community dubbed Secretariat the greatest thoroughbred since Man o' War retired in 1920. He was timed in 2:24, a new Belmont record and the fastest dirt-course mile and a half ever run in America.

Chris Evert first appeared on the world tennis scene as a 15-year-old when she upset Margaret Smith Court, 7–6, 7–6, shortly after Court had won the Grand Slam in 1970. A year later, Evert reached the U.S. Open semifinal, and by the end of the decade she had won the Open four times.

At age 18 in 1975 Nancy Lopez finished in a three-way tie for second in the U.S. Women's Open. Three years later she turned pro and won nine tournaments, including a record-setting five in a row. Eight more wins the next year gave her a second straight Player of the Year award.

1980–1989

In baseball, it's Willie Mays, 1954. In pro football, "The Catch" belongs to Dwight Clark, sending the 49ers to Super Bowl XVI.

1980–1989

The great rivalry of the eighties began on March 26, 1979, at the University of Utah's aptly named Special Events Center in Salt Lake City. Third-ranked Michigan State and number-one Indiana State met in the NCAA final, and the two best college basketball players in the country faced each other for the first time. From that night on, in the minds of sports fans, Magic Johnson and Larry Bird would always be a tandem. ❧ **Magic and the Spartans won** easily, 75–64, but the hype surrounding the game put the Madness in March and attracted more television viewers than had

Magic (left) and Bird, NCAA Finals

ever watched a college basketball game before. The NCAAs became an even bigger attraction in the eighties, when underdogs ran off with five championships, led by North Carolina State in 1983, Villanova in 1985, and Kansas in 1988.

ESPN, the newborn cable TV network that had loads of air time but little first-rate programming, quickly made a name for itself by picking up the early rounds of the tournament and feeding its growing audience of sports junkies and couch potatoes live and tape-delayed coverage around the clock. ❧ **But the real beneficiary** of the national interest surrounding Magic and Bird was the NBA, where charisma and teamwork were in short supply, TV ratings were in full retreat, and several franchises were in danger of folding. Magic and Bird changed a lot of that when they turned pro for the 1979–80 season. With Magic in Los Angeles ushering in Laker Showtime and Bird in Boston restoring Celtic Pride, the American public had a rooting interest in the

1980

JAN. 20
Ten seasons after going 1–13 in his first year as Steelers head coach, 48-year-old Chuck Noll guides Pittsburgh to an unprecedented fourth Super Bowl victory.

APR. 12
U.S. Olympic Committee endorses President Jimmy Carter's boycott of Moscow Summer Olympics to protest Soviet Union's December 1979 invasion of Afghanistan.

MAY 3
Genuine Risk outruns 12 colts to become only second filly to win Kentucky Derby in 106 years. First was Regret in 1915.

MAY 24
New York Islanders claim first Stanley Cup in six-game final with Philadelphia. For rookie defenseman Ken Morrow, lifting Cup comes exactly three months after winning gold medal in Lake Placid.

OCT. 2
Muhammad Ali, now 38, unretires to take on heavyweight champion Larry Holmes and suffers TKO in 11th round.

FEB. 22
Do you believe in miracles? U.S. Olympic hockey team topples mighty Soviet Union, 4–3, at Lake Placid. Seventh-seeded Americans go on to win first gold medal since 1960.

FEB. 23
American speed skater Eric Heiden completes sweep of all five men's gold medals with world record in 10,000 meters.

APR. 21
Bill Rodgers equals Clarence DeMar's record of three straight wins in Boston Marathon. Rosie Ruiz, the first woman across finish line, is revealed as a fraud and stripped of laurels.

MAY 16
Rookie Magic Johnson leads Los Angeles Lakers to NBA championship as Philadelphia 76ers fall in six games.

JULY 5
The world's two best tennis players, No. 1 Bjorn Borg and No. 2 John McEnroe, go five sets in Wimbledon final. Borg wins, 1–6, 7–5, 6–3, 6–7, 8–6, for fifth straight All-England title.

OCT. 21
After 77 years, Philadelphia Phillies finally win their first World Series. Kansas City Royals are defeated in six games.

NOV. 25
Five months after losing his WBC welterweight title to Roberto Duran on points, Sugar Ray Leonard wins it back when Duran inexplicably quits with Leonard ahead in eighth round.

1981

JAN. 25
Oakland Raiders defeat Philadelphia, 27–10, in New Orleans to become first wild-card team to win Super Bowl.

MAR. 30
Sophomore Isiah Thomas leads Indiana to NCAA title, beating North Carolina, 63–50.

JAN. 1
Unbeaten and top-ranked Georgia clinches first national championship with 17–10 victory over No. 7 Notre Dame in Sugar Bowl.

FEB. 15
Richard Petty wins Daytona 500 for seventh and final time. He has won the race in a Plymouth, Dodge, Oldsmobile, and now a Buick.

MAY 3
Trailing Philadelphia 3–1 in games, Larry Bird leads Boston comeback to win Eastern Conference finals in NBA playoffs. Celtics win championship series with Houston in six games.

OCT. 6
Baseball playoffs begin without Cincinnati Reds, who had the best season-long record (66–42) in majors but didn't win either the first or second half of the NL West.

JULY 31
Fifty-day baseball strike over free-agent compensation ends with 38 percent of schedule cancelled. Season will be divided into halves with extra round of divisional playoffs in postseason.

1982

MAR. 25
Wayne Gretzky picks up two goals and two assists against Calgary to become first NHL player to score 200 points in a single season. He scored the first 50 of his record 92 goals in 39 games.

MAR. 29
Jump shot by North Carolina freshman Michael Jordan beats Georgetown, 63–62, giving coach Dean Smith his first NCAA championship.

MAY 30
Gordon Johncock noses out Rick Mears by 16-hundreths of a second to win his second Indianapolis 500.

JUNE 20
Tom Watson wins U.S. Open at Pebble Beach after chipping in on 71st hole to break tie with Jack Nicklaus. A month later Watson claims his fourth British Open title.

JULY 4
Jimmy Connors wins his second Wimbledon singles title in a five-set struggle with John McEnroe that lasts over four hours. Two months later he will win his fourth U.S. Open.

JULY 11
Italy scores three goals in second half to beat West Germany, 3–1, in World Cup final at Madrid.

JULY 16
Mary Decker-Tabb sets world record of 31:35.30 in 10,000 meters, giving her four world marks (also mile, 3,000, and 5,000).

NOV. 16
NFL players' strike, called on Sept. 20 over new collective bargaining agreement, ends after 57 days. Regular season reduced from 16 games to nine. Sixteen teams will qualify for playoffs.

NOV. 20
University of California scores on five-lateral kickoff return in dying seconds to beat Stanford, 25–20. Some inadvertent downfield blocking is provided by Stanford band, which had taken field thinking game was over.

1983

JAN. 1
Second-ranked Penn State finally wins national championship, beating No. 1 Georgia, 27–23, in Sugar Bowl.

APR. 4
Heavily favored Houston is upset by No. 16 North Carolina State, 54–52, in NCAA title game. Last-second basket snaps Cougars' 26-game winning streak.

Fernando Valenzuela, fount of Fernandomania

NBA again. And, yes, it helped that Larry was that rare Bird indeed—a white superstar in a game dominated by blacks. 🐦 Four-time NBA All-Star Chris Mullin was a junior in high school when Magic and Bird joined the NBA. Years later he remembered their impact this way: "What they showed players and spectators was that you played hard on every play, every night, every season. You were unselfish and you were fundamentally sound. And if you did those things, you won." 🐦 Either Magic or Bird appeared in the NBA Finals every year of the eighties and on three occasions they played each other. The Lakers won five titles and the Celtics won three. Magic was named Most Valuable Player in the playoffs three times and Bird twice. But they had help. Magic never won a title without all-time NBA scoring leader Kareem Abdul-Jabbar, and Bird could always count on Kevin McHale and Robert Parish. 🐦 With the arrival of another superstar named Michael Jordan in 1984, the league's fortunes went nowhere but up. Attendance rebounded, four-year network TV contracts climbed from $88 million in 1982 to $600 million in 1990, and the league added five expansion teams. All that and a collective bargaining agreement with the players that included a salary cap. 🐦 The same autumn Magic and Bird made their joint debut in the NBA, two other super heroes known for their passing—hockey's Wayne Gretzky and football's Joe Montana—started their careers in the NHL and NFL, respectively. In the eighties, Gretzky led the Edmonton Oilers to four Stanley Cup championships and Montana quarterbacked the San Francisco 49ers to the same number of Super Bowls. 🐦 The 19-year-old Gretzky was an immediate sensation, coming over from the defunct World Hockey Association and tying for the scoring title with 50 goals and 137 points in his first try. In 1982 he became hockey's Babe Ruth, shattering the single-season record of 76 goals with 92. But he was just warming up. In his first 10 seasons, The Great One averaged 64 goals and 120 assists per year, and then, on October 15, 1989, he broke the all-time NHL career scoring record of 1,851 points that it took his idol Gordie Howe 26 years to establish. ❧ **Along the way The Great One** won the Hart Trophy as regular season MVP nine times in 10 years and, after his blockbuster trade to Los Angeles in 1988, turned one of the league's worst franchises into one of its most popular. "Hockey needed a shot in the arm when he came along," said former NHL and WHA great Bobby Hull, referring to the NHL's seventies reputation for fighting rather than scoring goals. "It needed a champion." ❧ **While Gretzky** was a sure thing, Montana was just a third-round pick out of Notre Dame in the 1979 NFL draft and the 82nd player chosen overall. Even he wasn't sure he'd make it until 49ers coach Bill Walsh made him the linchpin of the West Coast Offense at the end of his second season. The next year Montana led the league in passing and the Niners won their first Super Bowl. ❧ **In two games** separated by 10 years—the 1979 Cotton Bowl and the 1989 Super Bowl—Montana showed his uncanny ability to generate spectacular come-from-behind victories in the last minute, the second leading the Niners to another Super Bowl title. "He's got this resourcefulness," Walsh said once. "He won't choke. Or rather, if he ever does, you'll know everyone else has come apart first." ❧ **Not that some things didn't come a bit unglued** in the eighties. The players' unions in baseball and football both went out on strikes that lasted 50 days or more. In 1981, the baseball players struck over

MAY 28
Unseeded Kathy Horvath upsets Martina Navratilova in fourth round of French Open. It is the only match Martina loses all year and prevents her from winning the Grand Slam.

SEPT. 26
A foreign challenger finally wins America's Cup as *Australia II* beats *Liberty* in seventh and deciding race off Newport, R.I. Defeat is first for U.S. boat in 132 years of race.

FEB. 16
Bill Johnson, Steve Mahre, and Debbie Armstrong lead surprise U.S. ski team to five alpine medals in Winter Olympics at Sarajevo, Yugoslavia.

APR. 2
Georgetown wins only NCAA championship of Patrick Ewing era, beating Houston, 84–75, in Seattle.

JUNE 12
Boston wins first Bird vs. Magic showdown in NBA finals. Celtics 111, Lakers 102 in Game 7 at Boston Garden.

AUG. 3
American gymnast Mary Lou Retton, 16, registers perfect 10s in floor exercise and vault to win Olympic gold medal in all-around event.

MAY 31
Philadelphia wins NBA championship for first time in 16 years as 76ers sweep Lakers and dominate playoffs with 12–1 record.

1984

JAN. 1
Fifth-ranked Miami of Florida holds off late rally by No. 1 Nebraska to win Orange Bowl, 31–30. Loss by No. 2 Texas in Cotton Bowl allows Hurricanes to claim first national championship.

MARCH 29
NFL Colts evacuate Baltimore training facility under cover of darkness and move to Indianapolis where team will play in new 60,000-seat Hoosier Dome.

APR. 5
Kareem Abdul Jabbar becomes the NBA's all-time leading scorer, eclipsing Wilt Chamberlain's total of 31,419 points.

JULY 28
Summer Olympic Games open in Los Angeles without Soviet Union and 13 other Eastern Bloc countries that boycott in retaliation for U.S. leading walkout of 1980 Games in Moscow.

AUG. 11
Carl Lewis runs 8.94 anchor leg to cinch world record by U.S. Olympic 4x100 relay team. Gold medal is his fourth of Los Angeles Summer Games, tying him with Jesse Owens.

1985

APRIL 1
Unranked Villanova shocks top-ranked Georgetown, 66–64, to win All-Big East showdown in NCAA title game.

APR. 15
Middleweight champion Marvin Hagler knocks out challenger Thomas Hearns in third round of epic slugfest.

MAY 12
Kathy Whitworth wins LPGA stop in Portsmouth, Va., for 88th and final career victory, tops for men and women pros.

JUNE 9
After eight unsuccessful tries, dating back to 1959 when they still played in Minneapolis, the Lakers finally beat the Celtics in the NBA finals. Kareem Abdul-Jabbar, 38, is series MVP.

SEPT. 11
Cincinnati player-manager Pete Rose passes Ty Cobb as baseball's most prolific hitter. He lines base hit No. 4,192 off San Diego pitcher Eric Show and into left field at Riverfront Stadium.

SEPT. 21
Michael Spinks becomes first light heavyweight champion to win heavyweight title when he beats Larry Holmes in close, but unanimous, 15-round decision. Loss is first of Holmes' pro career.

1986

APR. 2
A year after NCAA introduces 45-second shot clock, college basketball adopts three-point field goal at a minimum distance of 19 feet, 9 inches from basket.

MAY 3
Ferdinand, a 17–1 longshot with a 54-year-old jockey and a 73-year-old trainer, wins Kentucky Derby. The victory is jockey Bill Shoemaker's fourth and trainer Charlie Whittingham's first.

JULY 27
America's Greg LeMond becomes first non-European cyclist to win Tour de France, beating defending champion Bernard Hinault of France by more than three minutes.

JULY 7
Boris Becker becomes youngest (17) and first unseeded player to win men's singles title at Wimbledon. He's also the first German.

JULY 7
Record 23-tournament winning streak of Martina Navratilova and doubles partner Pam Shriver ends in finals at Wimbledon where they lose to Kathy Jordan and Liz Smylie.

SEPT. 15
European team wins Ryder Cup matches at Sutton Coldfield, England. U.S. golfers lose for first time in 28 years.

OCTOBER
Kansas City Royals come back from 3–1 deficits in both AL playoffs against Toronto and World Series against St. Louis to win their first world championship.

JAN. 26
Chicago crushes New England by 36 points in Super Bowl XX. NFL title is Bears' first since 1963 when coach Mike Ditka was an all-pro tight end for George Halas.

APR. 13
Jack Nicklaus becomes oldest winner of Masters, claiming his sixth green blazer at age 46. Two months later, Ray Floyd becomes oldest winner of U.S. Open at 43.

JUNE 29
Led by Diego Maradona, Argentina wins second World Cup, beating West Germany, 3–2, in final at Mexico City.

JULY 27
Pat Bradley's victory in du Maurier Classic gives her three of LPGA's four majors in same calendar year. She won Nabisco Dinah Shore April 6, and LPGA Championship June 1.

At age 19 in 1988, Steffi Graf won the Grand Slam and the Olympic gold medal.

free-agent compensation and returned seven weeks later to play a bizarre split-season schedule that kept the Cincinnati Reds, the team with the best overall record in the majors, out of the playoffs. ✒ A **year later, NFL players** walked out for 57 days demanding a bigger slice of the league's new five-year, $2.1 billion contract with ABC, CBS, and NBC. They returned to the picket line in 1987 in a dispute over free agency, but the strike lost steam after 24 days when the owners kept the season going with replacement players and some of the strikers started returning to camp. The free agency issue would not be resolved for another five years. ✒ **Baseball, the NFL, and the NBA** all struggled with drug-abuse problems, the seriousness of which was apparent to all in 1986 with the cocaine-related deaths of Cleveland Browns defensive back Don Rogers and University of Maryland forward Len Bias, who was also the top draft pick of the NBA Celtics. The decade's most infamous abuser was Canadian sprinter Ben Johnson, who set a world record in the 100 meters at the 1988 Summer Olympics in Seoul and then flunked the post-race drug test for steroids. Johnson was sent packing but his gold medal stayed.

Ben Johnson sets a record at 100 meters, Seoul.

Greg LeMond (yellow jersey), Tour de France, 1986

❧ **Also banished were** Pete Rose and the win-at-all-costs football program at Southern Methodist University. Rose, who passed Ty Cobb as baseball's all-time hits leader in 1985, was barred for life in 1989 by Commissioner Bart Giamatti for betting on ballgames while managing the Reds. SMU was benched for the 1987 season and denied any scholarships for a year by the NCAA Committee on Infractions. The charge was repeated recruiting violations and illegal payments to players. The punishment was the first "death penalty" issued by the NCAA since Kentucky was expelled for the 1952–53 basketball season in the wake of a point-shaving scandal. ❧ **But the eighties were more about revival** than scandal. The 1980 U.S. Olympic hockey team and speed skater Eric Heiden restored America's faith in miracles and perseverance at the Lake Placid Winter Games. Golf's Ryder Cup came back to life when the British side was expanded to include all the best players in Europe and they held the United States even in the six biennial matches between 1979 and 1989. The luster returned to boxing's welterweight and middleweight divisions when Sugar Ray Leonard, Roberto Duran, Thomas Hearns, and Marvin Hagler all met each other in title fights and Leonard got the best of them. America's Cup yacht racing finally became a competitive affair in 1983 when Australia handed the U.S. its first loss in

OCT. 25
Even with a 3–2 edge in games, a 5–3 lead, and two outs and none on for the Mets in the bottom of the 10th, the Red Sox still can't win their first World Series since 1918. Three singles, a wild pitch, and a Bill Buckner error give New York the game. The Series is tied but it's over.

NOV. 22
Mike Tyson, 20, becomes youngest heavyweight champion ever, knocking out WBC titleholder Trevor Berbick in second round.

1987

JAN. 25
Trailing Denver 10–9 at halftime, New York Giants erupt for 30 points in second half to win their first Super Bowl.

FEB. 4
Dennis Connor, who lost the America's Cup to Australia in 1983, wins it back Down Under as skipper of *Stars & Stripes*. U.S. boat routs defender *Kookaburra III* in four straight races.

FEB. 25
NCAA sentences renegade football program at Southern Methodist University to "death penalty" for repeated rules violations, especially improper payments to players. SMU football will be effectively nonexistent for next two years.

APR. 6
Inactive for almost three years, Sugar Ray Leonard comes out of his latest retirement to beat world middleweight champion Marvin Hagler in a 12-round split decision.

JUNE 4
NCAA hurdles champion Danny Harris upsets world champion Edwin Moses in 400-meter hurdles at international meet in Madrid. Loss snaps Moses' 10-year, 122-race winning streak.

JUNE 14
Lakers and Celtics meet in NBA finals for third time in four years. Lakers win rubber match in six games.

SEPT. 15
Team Canada wins dramatic three-game Canada Cup finals against the Soviet Union as Wayne Gretzky and Mario Lemieux team up for winning goals in Games 2 and 3. First two games go into overtime and third is decided with 1:26 left in regulation.

SEPT. 27
Seve Ballesteros leads European golfers to second straight victory over U.S. in Ryder Cup. Win is first on American soil for Euros.

OCT. 25
NFL season resumes after 24-day players' strike over free agency. Regular season reduced from 16 games to 15 when one weekend was canceled, but three weekends played with replacement players.

OCT. 25
Minnesota Twins win first World Series since leaving Washington, D.C., in 1961. St. Louis beaten, 4–2, in Game 7 at Metrodome, the first indoor venue in Series history.

1988

FEB. 14
At the Winter Olympics in Calgary, Matti Nykanen of Finland wins both the 70- and 90-meter ski jumps while Great Britain's clownish "Eddie the Eagle" Edwards finishes last in both events.

MARCH
Susan Butcher, a breeder and trainer of Alaskan huskies, wins her third straight Iditarod Trail Sled Dog Race, covering the 1,151-mile Northern Route in a record 11 days and 11 hours.

AUG. 9
Edmonton Oilers trade Wayne Gretzky to Los Angeles after nine seasons, eight MVP awards, seven scoring titles, and four Stanley Cup championships.

SEPT. 29
Florence Griffith Joyner (200 meters) and sister-in-law Jackie Joyner Kersee (long jump) both win Olympic gold medals. They will leave Seoul with five golds and one silver between them, a better haul than 136 of 159 competing countries.

OCT. 15
Limping Kirk Gibson of Dodgers belts pinch-hit, two-run homer off Oakland's Dennis Eckersley in bottom of ninth to win Game 1 of World Series. L.A. wins title in five games.

JUNE 21
Lakers beat Detroit Pistons, 108–105, in Game 7 of NBA finals, becoming league's first repeat champions since Celtics in 1969.

AUG. 8
Sun sets on last ballpark without lights as Wrigley Field hosts first night game between Cubs and visiting Phillies. Rain intervenes, however, and game is postponed after 3 1/2 innings.

SEPT. 24
Ben Johnson of Canada wins Olympic 100-meter dash in world-record time of 9.79 then flunks urine test and is sent home in disgrace. Defending champion Carl Lewis (9.92) gets gold.

OCT. 1
Steffi Graf beats Gabriela Sabatini in straight sets at Summer Olympics in Seoul to become first tennis player to win Grand Slam and a gold medal in same calendar year.

1989

FEB. 19
Three-time Winston Cup champion Darrell Waltrip wins his first Daytona 500 on fumes after going last 132.5 miles without refueling.

JAN. 22
Joe Montana engineers 11-play, 92-yard touchdown drive with 3:10 remaining to lead 49ers past Cincinnati, 20–16, in Super Bowl XXIII. MVP, however, is Jerry Rice, who catches 11 passes for 215 yards on a sprained ankle.

JUNE 5
The same weekend pro-democracy demonstrations are being crushed at Tiananmen Square in Beijing, Chinese-American Michael Chang wins French Open and remembers protesters in his victory speech.

JULY 22
Trailing overall leader Laurent Fignon by 50 seconds with one time trial to go, Greg LeMond catches Fignon with eight seconds to spare and wins his second Tour de France.

SEPT. 1
Baseball commissioner Bart Giamatti, 51, dies of a heart attack eight days after banning Pete Rose from the game for life. Giamatti found Rose guilty of betting on major league games.

OCT. 17
An earthquake measuring 7.1 on the Richter scale hits Bay Area immediately before start of Game 3 in San Francisco–Oakland World Series. After 10-day postponement, Series resumes and A's complete four-game sweep.

Cricket heroes Ian Botham of England (left) and Viv Richards of the West Indies

132 years and the Americans responded by sailing Down Under four years later and winning the Cup back. And Greg LeMond recalled America's turn-of-the-century love affair with bicycles by becoming the first U.S. rider to win the Tour de France in 1987 and then recovering from a hunting accident to win twice more in 1989 and 1990. 🦋

Political boycotts buffeted the Summer Olympics between 1976 and 1984, particularly the Moscow Games in 1980 when an American-led walkout over the Russian invasion of Afghanistan resulted in 64 Western nations staying away. The Soviets, who spent nearly $9 billion on their games, retaliated four years later by getting 14 Eastern Bloc countries to shun Los Angeles and the plans of Peter Ueberroth and his organizing committee to run the first games ever financed privately. 🦋

Ueberroth's corporate Olympics showed the Lords of the Rings that the games could pay their own way, and then some. With minimal construction costs, expenses were pegged at $500 million and funded primarily through TV contracts, commercial sponsorships, and ticket sales. Nothing was free. When it was all over, and Carl Lewis and Joan Benoit and Mary Lou Retton were household names, the 1984 Olympic fortnight had turned a staggering profit of more than $220 million—all of which went to support amateur sports in southern California and the rest of the country. 🦋 **That fall, Ueberroth** was named commissioner of baseball, where his management skills were sorely needed in restoring the major leagues to financial good health. His success in this regard was called into question several years later when his organized effort to help owners keep costs down was judged to be collusion against the players' union and cost the owners $280 million in damages. 🦋

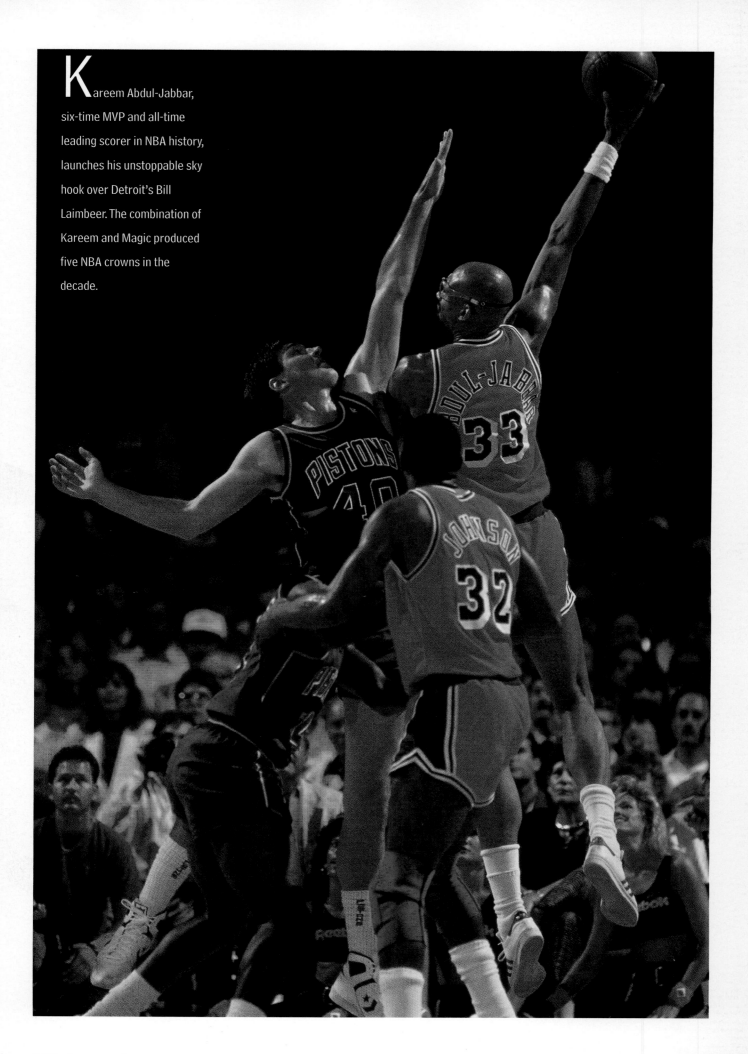

Kareem Abdul-Jabbar, six-time MVP and all-time leading scorer in NBA history, launches his unstoppable sky hook over Detroit's Bill Laimbeer. The combination of Kareem and Magic produced five NBA crowns in the decade.

S wooping and soaring, Julius Erving pioneered a new style of play—above the rim and in your face—in the

raucous days of the American Basketball Association. Though his floor-length forays dwindled in the conservative NBA,

he remained uniquely "Dr. J."

Under skipper Richard Brown in 1851, the clipper *America* defeated 14 of England's finest vessels in a race around the Isle of Wight and gave name to the America's Cup. The United States retained the Cup against 24 successive challenges until September 26, 1983, when *Australia II* (above) defeated Dennis Conner's *Liberty*. Conner reclaimed the Cup in 1987 (right) as *Stars and Stripes* defeated *Kookaburra III*.

ayne Gretzky and the Edmonton Oilers joined the NHL with three other WHA refugees in the fall of 1979. Within nine seasons, Gretzky had eight league scoring titles and the Oilers had four Stanley Cup championships. They won their first Cup in 1984 by ending the four-year reign of Denis Potvin and the New York Islanders (below).

Joe Montana takes off against the Cincinnati Bengals in Super Bowl XXIII. Trailing 16–13 with 3:10 to play, Montana led his 49ers on a characteristic 11-play, 92-yard drive to the winning touchdown. He quarterbacked in four Super Bowls and won them all, throwing for 11 touchdowns and no interceptions.

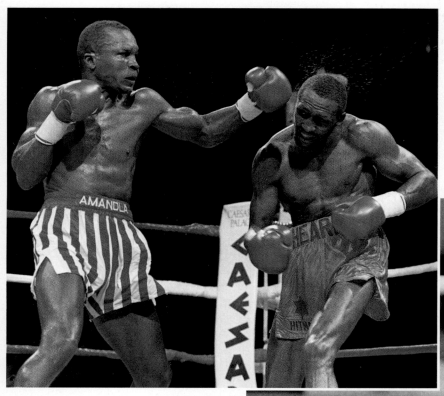

Sugar Ray Leonard (striped trunks) and Thomas Hearns were already acclaimed two of the greatest boxers of all time when they met on June 12, 1989, for their third bout in the 1980s. Leonard had previously captured world titles in five distinct weight classifications—the most ever—and Hearns would go on after this fight (a 12-round draw) to gain his fourth.

Jack Nicklaus came to the 1986 Masters as a five-time winner with a record 19 major championships. But at the age of 46, the Golden Bear had his eyes on one last Masters title. Here he watches a birdie roll in on the 17th green on the final day.

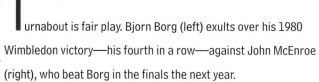

Turnabout is fair play. Bjorn Borg (left) exults over his 1980 Wimbledon victory—his fourth in a row—against John McEnroe (right), who beat Borg in the finals the next year.

The 17-year-old Boris Becker was a sensation when he took Wimbledon in 1985, flinging himself across the court with disregard for personal safety. In the 1980s he won two more All-England titles, plus a U.S. Open.

Simply the best. Not only did Martina Navratilova take 18 Grand Slam singles and 38 Grand Slam doubles titles, she retired with more tournament victories (167) than any other man or woman who ever played the game. Here she powers her way to her sixth straight Wimbledon title of the nine she would win overall.

In Game 6 of the 1986 World Series, Bill Buckner of Boston booted a grounder by Mookie Wilson (right), which permitted Ray Knight to score. Twelve times in that nightmarish 10th inning, the Red Sox were one pitch away from wiping out the Curse of the Bambino.

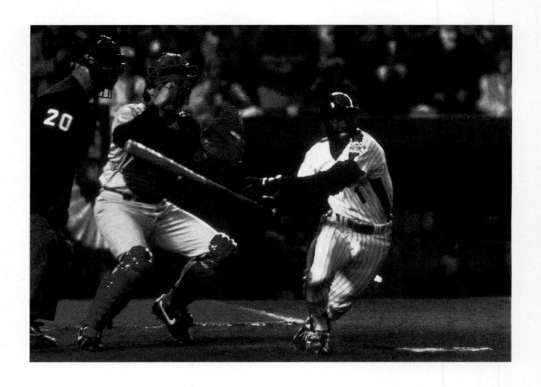

The Wizard of Oz, Ozzie Smith, displays the acrobatic skills that made him, by universal acclaim, the best-fielding shortstop ever.

The Thief of Baghdad, Rickey Henderson, steals one of his record 130 bases in 1982. Beginning his two-decades-plus career with the Oakland A's, Rickey proceeded to surpass Lou Brock as baseball's single-season and all-time stolen-base king.

Speed skater Eric Heiden won five individual gold medals at the 1988 Winter Olympics in Lake Placid, the most anyone—winter or summer games—has ever won. He set Olympic records in all five events he entered, and set a world mark in the 10,000-meter race.

Gymnast Mary Lou Retton became America's sweetheart with her winning smile, but it was her strength and her competitive edge that won her five medals at the 1984 Olympics.

Italy's charismatic and flamboyant Alberto Tomba became the first alpine skier to take slalom events in consecutive Olympics when he won the slalom and giant slalom in 1988 and followed with another giant slalom in 1992.

Jackie Joyner-Kersee (right) soared to gold medals in both the long jump and heptathlon at the 1988 Summer Olympics in Seoul. Florence Griffith-Joyner, her sister-in-law, won three golds at Seoul in the 100-meter run, 200-meter run, and 4 x 100-meter relay. Each won a Sullivan Award as amateur athlete of the year.

Carl Lewis in 1984 at Los Angeles, defying space and time. The amazing Lewis won nine gold medals over four Olympiads (1984–96), including four successive long jump competitions.

1990–1999

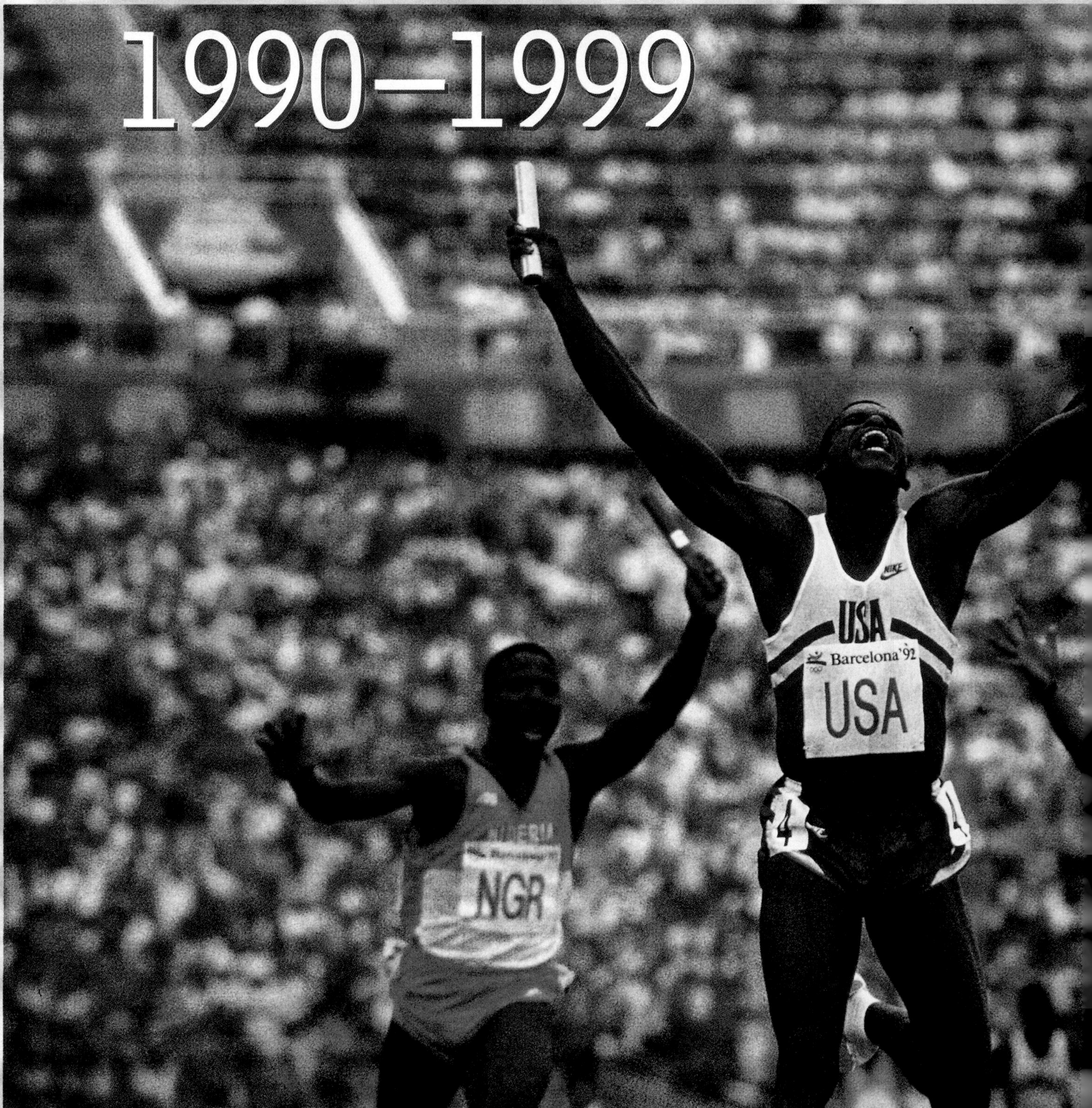

Silver and bronze medal winners rejoice, but Carl Lewis clinches the gold in the 4 x 100-meter relay at Barcelona.

1990–1999

1990

The decade wasn't quite two years old when the Soviet Union officially ceased to exist on December 25, 1991. Its demise followed the reunification of East and West Germany by 14 months and ended Communist rule not only in Eastern Europe but in the Olympics as well. ❧ **For 40 years**—from their 1952 Olympic debut in Helsinki to their curtain call as a Unified Team of 12 former republics in Barcelona—the Soviets finished first in the national medal standings 15 times and runner-up five times in the 20 Winter and Summer Games they attended. Over the same period, the United States was first or second in medals won just 11 times, all but two of those in the summer. ❧ **East Germany had risen** to challenge the USSR in the seventies as the world's foremost state-supported sports machine and even out-medaled its mentor at Lake Placid in 1980. A reunited Germany—minus coaches from the East who were viewed as notorious purveyors of performance-enhancing drugs—and the new Russia remained at or near the top of the international ladder in the nineties, but a significant chapter in Olympic history had closed. ❧ **Russia also exported its** best hockey players to the NHL, where six of them helped the Detroit Red (Army) Wings win back-to-back Stanley Cup championships in 1997 and 1998. In fact, three players from former Communist countries, Sergei Federov of Russia, and Dominik Hasek and Jaromir Jagr of the Czech Republic, combined to win four Hart Trophies as the league's MVP from 1994 to 1999. Hasek and Jagr also led the Czechs to a 1–0 victory over Russia in 1998 at Nagano to claim their first Olympic hockey gold medal. ❧ **The International Olympic Committee** opened the door to professional athletes at the 1992 Summer Games in Barcelona

JAN. 28
San Francisco flattens Denver, 55–10, in most one-sided victory in Super Bowl history. Only NFL championship games of 1940 (Chicago Bears 73, Washington 0) and 1954 (Cleveland 56, Detroit 10) were bigger title-game routs.

FEB. 10
Buster Douglas pulls off boxing upset of century with 10th-round knockout of unbeaten heavyweight champion Mike Tyson in Tokyo. Douglas was such a long shot, Tyson was favored 42 to 1.

APR. 9
Baseball season opens one week late after new collective bargaining agreement is reached following 32-day lockout of spring training camps.

MAY 24
Edmonton Oilers beat Boston in five games to win fifth Stanley Cup in seven years and first without Wayne Gretzky.

JUNE 10
U.S. national soccer team is trounced, 5–1, by Czechoslovakia in its first World Cup tournament appearance in 40 years.

JUNE
Tennis player Monica Seles becomes youngest winner of French Open at 16, and golfer Hale Irwin becomes oldest player to win U.S Open at 45.

JULY 7
Martina Navratilova beats Zina Garrison, 6–4, 6–1, to win Wimbledon singles title a record ninth time. She had been tied at eight with Helen Wills Moody.

OCT. 25
The reign of Buster Douglas as heavyweight champion of the world ends after eight and a half months when Evander Holyfield knocks him out in the third round.

1991

JAN. 27
New York Giants win first one-point Super Bowl, 20–19. Buffalo place-kicker Scott Norwood misses 47-yard field goal attempt with eight seconds left.

APR. 1
Duke finally wins NCAA basketball title in ninth trip to Final Four. Blue Devils beat undefeated UNLV, 79–77, in semifinals and Kansas, 72–65, in final.

APR. 19
Evander Holyfield defends heavyweight title against 42-year-old, 257-pound former champion George Foreman and wins unanimous 12-round decision. Foreman was 24–0 since hitting comeback trail in 1987 after 10 years of retirement.

MAY 1
Nolan Ryan, 44, who became oldest pitcher to throw a no-hitter in 1990, hurls seventh and final gem of his 25-year career. He also fans 16 as Texas beats Toronto, 3–0.

MAY 25
Mario Lemieux leads Pittsburgh Penguins to first Stanley Cup title in six-game series with Minnesota. Penguins' Bob Johnson becomes first coach to win both NCAA and NHL championships.

JUNE 12
Michael Jordan and Bulls claim first NBA championship, ousting Magic Johnson and Lakers from finals in five games.

Barcelona Olympics, 1992

AUG. 30
Mike Powell breaks Bob Beamon's 23-year-old long jump world record with a leap of 29 feet, 4^1/$_2$ inches at World Track and Field Championships in Tokyo. Runner-up Carl Lewis also sets a new world record of 9.86 seconds in 100-meter dash.

OCT. 27
Minnesota's Jack Morris pitches 10-inning, 1–0 shutout against Atlanta in Game 7 to earn Twins second World Series title in five years.

NOV. 7
Magic Johnson announces he has HIV virus that causes AIDS and is retiring from pro basketball at age 32. Earlier in year Arthur Ashe disclosed he had contracted HIV from a blood transfusion during a 1983 heart operation.

NOV. 30
U.S. women's national soccer team defeats Norway, 2–1, in China to win first Women's World Cup.

DEC. 1
France beats U.S. in Lyon to win Davis Cup championship for first time since reign of Four Musketeers from 1927–32.

1992

JAN. 26
Washington Redskins beat Buffalo, 37–24, to win third Super Bowl in 10 years with third different starting quarterback. In order: Joe Theismann, Doug Williams, and Mark Rypien.

FEB. 2–23
At Winter Olympics in Albertville, France, reunified Germany and temporarily united former republics of USSR finish 1–2 in team standings. All five U.S. gold medals are won by women, led by speed skater Bonnie Blair, who wins twice.

FEB. 16
Davey Allison wins Daytona 500, following tire tracks of father Bobby, who won race three times from 1978 to '88. Three months later, Al Unser Jr. will win Indianapolis 500, a race his dad won four times from 1970 to '87.

MAR. 10
Duke routs Michigan by 20 points to become first repeat champion in men's NCAA basketball tournament since UCLA won seven in a row, 1967–73.

APR. 6
Baseball season opens with President George Bush throwing out first pitch at Baltimore's new Camden Yards ballpark, first of "new classic" parks that are asymmetrical and for baseball only.

AUG. 2
Jackie Joyner-Kersee wins second straight heptathlon gold medal at Summer Olympics in Barcelona.

AUG. 8
Dream Team of NBA All-Stars, led by Magic Johnson, romps to Olympic gold medal, winning eight games by an average of 44 points.

AUG. 9
Barcelona Games close with Unified Team claiming one last Olympic team victory for old Soviet republics, out-medaling the U.S., 112–108. Germany is third with 82 medals.

OCT. 24
Toronto Blue Jays take World Series trophy north of border for first time, beating Atlanta in six games.

when the world's best basketball players were allowed to compete. It was 79 years after the International Olympic Committee stripped Jim Thorpe of his gold medals for playing two summers of semi-pro baseball. America's "Dream Team" of all-NBA multimillionaires was the sensation of the games. Fans and media from around the world flocked to get a look at Michael Jordan, Magic Johnson, Larry Bird, and company. Magic was doubly fascinating because in a world terrified by AIDS he had come out of retirement eight months after announcing he was HIV positive. Encountering more hero-worship than competition, the Dream Teamers easily won the gold medal. ✍ **IOC president** and hometown product Juan Antonio Samaranch basked in the festival atmosphere of the Barcelona Games, which many considered the most extraordinary ever held. There was no boycott for the first time in 20 years, a record 172 nations sent teams, South Africa was allowed back following the 1991 repudiation of apartheid by its white minority government, and professionals mixed easily with amateurs. ✍ **The Olympics boom** of the nineties was aided by advancing the Winter Games cycle to 1994 so that they would alternate every two years with the Summer Games. The peak came in 1995 when NBC completed a $3.5 billion deal to acquire the television broadcast rights to all five Olympics from 2000 to 2008. But the public relations bubble burst in 1999, when it was revealed that widespread corruption had tainted the IOC's procedures for selecting host cities,

Downhill skier Hermann Maier goes horizontal at Nagano.

especially Salt Lake City, the site of the 2002 Winter Games. Samaranch, who was 78 years old when the disclosures were made, vowed to clean up the mess but refused to consider resigning. ❧ **Former Olympic and world** heavyweight champion George Foreman didn't opt for the rocking chair either in the nineties. He regained the world title in 1994 by knocking out Michael Moorer in 10 rounds—a victory that not only made him the oldest heavyweight champion ever at age 45, but came 20 years and six days after he had lost the title to Muhammad Ali in the "Rumble in the Jungle" in Zaire. Both fights made the winners Associated Press Male Athletes of the Year, Ali in 1974 and Foreman in '94. ❧ **Don King, the electric-haired** high priest of hyperbole and elusive target of federal investigators, promoted the Zaire fight and soon became boxing's de facto chief executive through his association with Ali. A former numbers

The Bite

runner who did four years for manslaughter in the late sixties and early seventies, King spent the nineties cleaning up after Mike Tyson, who lost the heavyweight title twice, served a three-year prison term for rape, another three and a half months for assault, and had his boxing license revoked for 15 months after biting both of champion Evander Holyfield's ears in a 1997 title bout. ❧ **Michael Jordan quit playing** basketball twice during the decade, both times after leading the Bulls to three straight NBA championships. The first time, he took a year and a half off following the 1992–93 season because he wanted to give baseball a try. The second time, in 1999, he had nothing left to prove—not after a

1993

JAN. 31
Dallas reaches Super Bowl for first time since 1979 and wins for first time since 1978. Cowboys beat Buffalo badly, 52–17.

APR. 14
Mario Lemieux wins fourth NHL scoring title despite undergoing two months of radiation treatment to battle Hodgkin's disease.

MAY 11
U.S. Olympic Committee announces incentive payment for athletes: $15,000 for every gold medal, $10,000 for silver, $7,500 for bronze, and $5,000 for finishing fourth.

OCT. 6
Michael Jordan announces retirement from pro basketball at age 30, but leaves door open for return.

NOV. 14
Miami Dolphins coach Don Shula wins his 325th game, replacing George Halas as NFL's all-time leader in career victories.

MAR. 4
Sheryl Swoopes of Texas Tech scores record 47 points to lead Red Raiders to 84–82 victory over Ohio State in NCAA women's basketball tournament.

APR. 30
Monica Seles, the world's top-ranked female tennis player, is stabbed in back by a crazed Steffi Graf fan at tournament in Hamburg. Though not wounded seriously, Seles cannot play without pain for the rest of the year.

SEPT. 8–13
Chinese runners Qu Yunxia (1,500 meters) and Wang Junxia (3,000 and 10,000 meters) shatter three world records in six days. Wang's time of 29:31.78 in 10,000 betters old mark by 42 seconds.

NOV. 6
Evander Holyfield reclaims heavyweight crown, winning 12-round split decision against champion Riddick Bowe, who kept title warm for 51 weeks.

1994

FEBRUARY
Winter Olympics moved up to alternate with Summer Games every two years. Norway triumphant in Lillehammer, while U.S. speed skaters Bonnie Blair and Dan Jansen shine.

APR. 10
Jose Maria Olazabal of Spain wins Masters, sixth foreigner to claim golf's green blazer in last seven years.

JULY 17
Brazil beats Italy on penalty kicks to win World Cup an unprecedented fourth time. Tournament, held in U.S., breaks all attendance records and Americans' first-round victory over Colombia is national team's first in World Cup since 1950.

JAN. 1
Coach Bobby Bowden and Florida State finally win national championship as No. 1 Seminoles beat No. 2 Nebraska, 18–16, in Orange Bowl.

MAR. 23
Wayne Gretzky becomes NHL's all-time leading goal-scorer, passing Gordie Howe with goal No. 802.

JUNE 14
New York Rangers beat Vancouver, 3–2, in Game 7 to win Stanley Cup for first time since 1940. Two days later, Sergei Fedorov of Detroit becomes first Russian to win Hart Trophy as NHL's most valuable player.

AUG. 8
Indianapolis Motor Speedway hosts first NASCAR event. A crowd of 300,000 turns out to see Jeff Gordon win inaugural Brickyard 400.

NOV. 5
Twenty years after losing his heavyweight championship to Muhammad Ali in Zaire, 45-year-old George Foreman reclaims title in Las Vegas, knocking out Michael Moorer in 10th round.

JAN. 29
Steve Young tosses record six touchdown passes as San Francisco routs San Diego, 49–26, in first all-California Super Bowl in Miami. Niners have now won five Super Bowls.

MAR. 31
Baseball's 1994–95 strike ends after 232 days when federal judge issues injunction restoring terms of old collective bargaining agreement. Opening Day reset for April 25, regular season reduced from 162 to 144 games.

JUNE 24
With President Nelson Mandela looking on, South Africa defeats New Zealand, 15–12, to win Rugby World Cup final in Johannesburg. Tournament is first international competition hosted by South Africa since government renounced apartheid in 1991.

AUG. 12
Baseball players go on strike rather than accept owners' demand for a salary cap. Two months later the World Series, which had made it through two world wars and the Great Depression, is canceled for first time since 1904.

1995

JAN. 11
NHL owners' lockout over salary cap and luxury tax to benefit small market teams ends after 103 days. Regular-season schedule reduced from 84 to 48 games.

MAR. 19
Michael Jordan returns to NBA after 17 months off, scores 19 points as Bulls beat Indiana.

APR. 2
University of Connecticut women beat Tennessee, 70–64, to win their first NCAA basketball title and complete 35–0 season.

OCT. 3
Former football star O.J. Simpson found not guilty by a Los Angeles jury of murdering his ex-wife and her male friend.

OCT. 28
Atlanta beats Cleveland in six games for Braves' first World Series title since moving down south in 1966.

1996

JAN. 28
In battle of four-time champions, Dallas Cowboys beat Pittsburgh Steelers, 27–17, in Super Bowl XXX at Tempe, Ariz.

JAN. 2
No. 1-ranked Nebraska clobbers No. 2 Florida, 62–24, becoming first back-to-back national champions since Alabama in 1978–79.

MAR. 16
Former heavyweight champion Mike Tyson, released from jail a year ago after serving three years for rape, wins back WBC portion of title by knocking out Frank Bruno in three rounds.

Two three-peats

13-year career that included 10 scoring titles, six NBA playoff MVP awards, five regular season MVPs, and an annual salary of $35 million, plus more than that in endorsement deals. ❧ **The best sports marketing fit of the century** was Jordan's feet in Phil Knight's sneakers. Knight signed Jordan to a Nike endorsement contract during his NBA rookie year in 1984. He then brought out the revolutionary air-cushioned Air Jordans in 1985, ran lavish and ubiquitous TV commercials of a perpetually airborne Jordan, and the public was soon hooked on both Michael and anything that had a "swoosh" on it. Knight made billions—"the greatest fortune ever from athletics," according to Frank Deford of *Sports Illustrated.* ❧ **Jordan's second retirement** came on January 13, 1999, a month shy of his 36th birthday and a week after the end of a rancorous 191-day owners' lockout that shortened the 1998–99 season to 50 games in 90 days. The lockout ended with the NBA the only one of the four major pro leagues with a clearly defined cap on individual salaries. Back in 1983 when several NBA teams were in danger of folding, Commissioner David Stern and former players' union executive secretary Larry Fleisher agreed to pro sports' first salary cap, which guaranteed players 53 percent of gross revenues. ❧ **Baseball went through** the longest work stoppage in the history of professional sports in 1994, when the players' union rejected owners' demands for a salary cap and an end to salary arbitration. The players went on strike August 12 and didn't return until 232 days later when a federal judge prevented the owners from starting the 1995 season with replacement players.

The strike wiped out the remainder of the 1994 regular season; canceled the World Series, which had been played continuously since 1905; and shortened the 1995 season by three weeks. Interleague play was also adopted for 1997, but disillusioned fans didn't return in numbers equal to the 1993 season until the summer of '98 when Mark McGwire beat Sammy Sosa, 70–66, in the great home run race and the Yankees won the most regular-season games (114) in 92 years. History repeated itself—77 years after Babe Ruth saved baseball from the Black Sox scandal, home runs and the Yankees came to the rescue again.

The nineties had a certain dêjà vú quality, best seen in the popularity of golf's lucrative Senior PGA Tour, where the age minimum is 50, but the name recognition factor is high. The century's greatest golfer, Jack Nicklaus, became eligible in 1990 and won all four Senior major tournaments within two years. But he preferred to compete on the regular tour, where he had won a staggering 18 majors and finished second in 19 more from 1962 to 1986. In tennis, Pete Sampras and Martina Navratilova, the all-time money winners of the Open Era, cemented their reputations on the game's original grass surface by setting

Sampras at Wimbledon

new records for 20th-century singles championships at Wimbledon—nine for Navratilova and six for Sampras. And in auto racing, the Indianapolis Motor Speedway, which held its first 500-mile,

APR. 15
In 100th running of Boston Marathon, Moses Tanui of Kenya and Uta Pippig of Germany are the winners. Last Americans to win were Greg Meyer in 1983 and Lisa Laresen Weidenbach in 1985.

JUNE 16
Michael Jordan and the Bulls win their fourth NBA title of the decade, ending year with record 87 wins: 72–10 record during regular season and 15–3 in playoffs.

AUG. 4
Summer Olympics close with a record 77 nations winning at least one medal. In track, Michael Johnson sweeps 200- and 400-meter races and Carl Lewis wins fourth straight long jump title, tying discus thrower Al Oerter (1956–68) for consecutive victories.

JUNE 10
The Colorado Avalanche, who were the Quebec Nordiques a year before, win Stanley Cup in four-game sweep over Florida. Three weeks later, another Canadian-based former WHA champion, the Winnipeg Jets, moves to Phoenix and becomes the Coyotes.

JULY 19
Summer Olympics open in Atlanta with Muhammad Ali lighting flame to start games. A record 197 nations are in attendance, but not the Soviet Union.

SEPT. 29
Baseball regular season ends with 16 players hitting 40 or more home runs. Previous record was eight, set in 1961.

NOV. 9
Evander Holyfield knocks out Mike Tyson in 11th round to take Tyson's portion of the heavyweight championship.

1997

JAN. 26
Green Bay returns to Super Bowl after 29-year absence and throttles New England, 35–21. Packers won first two AFL–NFL World Championship Games before event became known as the Super Bowl.

APR. 13
Tiger Woods, 21, not only becomes youngest golfer and first black to win Masters, but also does it with lowest score (270) and by largest margin (12 strokes) ever.

AUG. 26
Michael Jordan agrees to play 1997–98 season with Bulls for $35 million. It will turn out to be his final season.

MAR. 22
Fourteen-year-old Tara Lipinski overtakes Sonja Henie as youngest figure skater to win a world championship. Lipinski is a month younger than Henie was when she won first of her 10 world titles in 1927.

JUNE 28
Mike Tyson, who lost his portion of the heavyweight title to Evander Holyfield the previous November, is disqualified in third round of rematch when he bites Holyfield's ears not once, but twice.

SEPT. 5
International Olympic Committee names Athens, Greece, as host city for 2004 Summer Games. Athens hosted very first modern Olympic Games in 1896.

OCT. 26
Five years after entering the National League as an expansion team, Florida Marlins win World Series in seven games over Cleveland. The Indians haven't won Series since 1948.

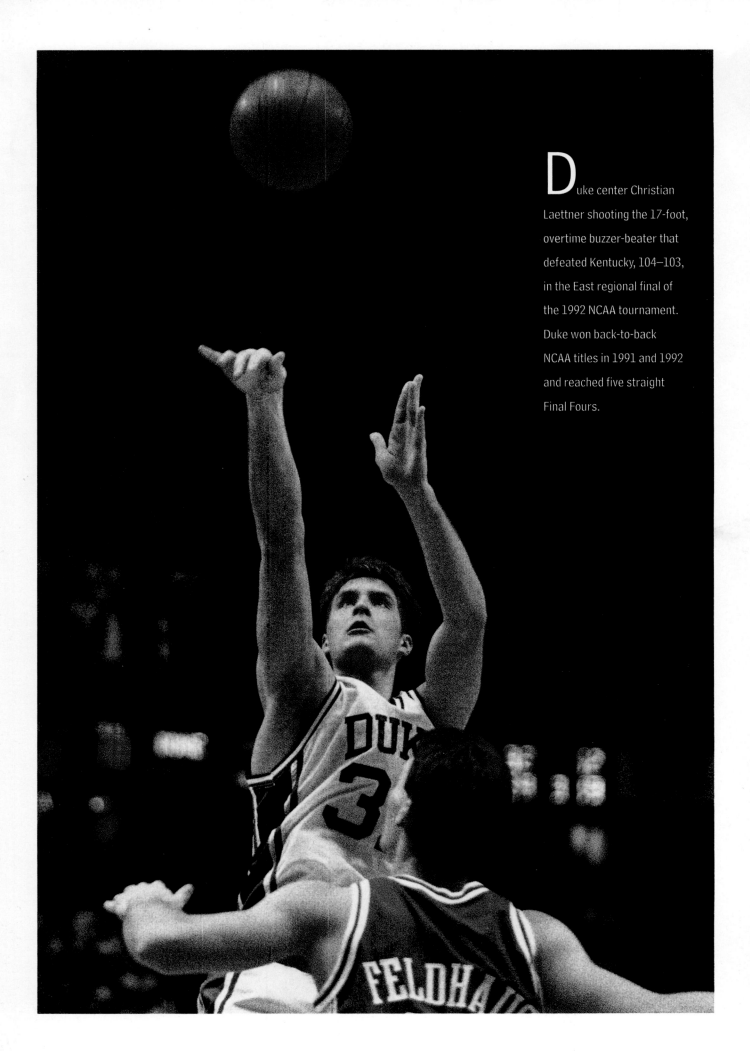

Duke center Christian Laettner shooting the 17-foot, overtime buzzer-beater that defeated Kentucky, 104–103, in the East regional final of the 1992 NCAA tournament. Duke won back-to-back NCAA titles in 1991 and 1992 and reached five straight Final Fours.

New York Rangers goaltender Mike Richter makes a spectacular glove save to preserve a 3–2 lead over Vancouver late in Game 7 of the 1994 Stanley Cup finals. Holding off the Canucks before a roaring full house at Madison Square Garden, the Rangers won the Cup for the first time in 54 years.

Unheralded Buster Douglas delivered the most unexpected knockout punch of the century on February 10, 1990, sending undefeated heavyweight champion Mike Tyson to the canvas in the 10th round of their title fight in Tokyo. Douglas entered the ring as a 42-to-1 long shot.

West Indian batsman Brian Lara knocks in another four, on his way to a world-record innings of 501 not out while playing for Warwickshire in a country cricket match against Durham, on June 6, 1994, at Edgbaston.

David Campese of Australia (left) is the most prolific winger ever to play international rugby. As a team, New Zealand's All-Blacks are considered the best in the world, although their pre-game Haka challenge (below) did not intimidate South Africa's Springboks, who won 15–12 in the finals of the 1995 Rugby World Cup.

Brandi Chastain loses her shirt after clinching the Women's World Cup championship with a penalty-kick goal against China on July 10, 1999. The Cup final was witnessed by more than 90,000 fans at the Rose Bowl in Pasadena and millions more on television.

Eighteen-year-old English striker Michael Owen cuts in front of Colombia's Wilmer Cabrera in a first-round game of the 1998 World Cup. Owen scored a sensational goal in the next round against Argentina, but the English were eliminated on penalty kicks.

Two days after winning his third straight U.S. Amateur championship in 1996 (above), 20-year-old Tiger Woods turned pro, signed two multi-million-dollar endorsement deals, and joined the PGA Tour. Seven months later he became the youngest player to win the Masters.

Payne Stewart winning his second U.S. Open of the decade, on June 20, 1999, at Pinehurst. Stewart, the only PGA Tour regular to commonly wear plus-fours, was a runner-up in 1993 and 1998.

Fred Couples blasts out of an 18th hole sand trap on the way to winning his first major title, the 1992 Masters. In the seven years from 1988 through 1994, Couples was the only American golfer to win at Augusta, as green blazers were issued to Sandy Lyle of England, Nick Faldo of England (twice), Ian Woosnam of Wales, Bernhard Langer of Germany, and Jose Maria Olazabal of Spain.

Cancer survivor Lance Armstrong returned to the international cycling circuit in 1999 to become the second American to win the Tour de France. He won the three-week, 2,300-mile race at a record average speed of 25 miles per hour.

Tennessee center Daedra Charles drives past Virginia's Heidi Burge for a layup in the 1991 NCAA championship game. The Vols beat the Cavaliers, 70–67, in overtime to win the first of their four titles in the nineties.

Pete Sampras began the nineties by beating Andre Agassi in straight sets to win the 1990 U.S. Open at age 19. He ended the decade by beating Agassi again in straight sets to win Wimbledon for the sixth time. Sampras shares the record for most Grand Slam singles titles with Australia's Roy Emerson, with 12.

Jim Kelly just gets a pass off before being dropped by Dallas linebacker Ken Norton in Super Bowl XXVII in Pasadena. Kelly was injured when Norton landed on his knee, and had to leave the game, sending the Bills' offense into a nine-turnover tailspin in a 52–17 defeat.

Jerry Rice (left) was the NFL's greatest receiver of the nineties, setting career records for catches and touchdowns. Buffalo placekicker Scott Norwood had an opportunity to leave his mark on the decade in the last seconds of Super Bowl XXV, but had the misfortune of seeing his 47-yard field goal drift wide right.

Gail Devers of the U.S. won gold medals in the 100-meter dash in the Olympics of 1992 and 1996. She also excelled as a hurdler at the IAAF World Championships with 100-meter titles in 1993, 1995, and 1999.

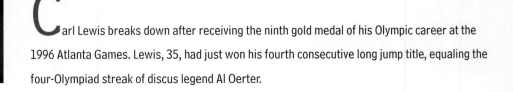

Carl Lewis breaks down after receiving the ninth gold medal of his Olympic career at the 1996 Atlanta Games. Lewis, 35, had just won his fourth consecutive long jump title, equaling the four-Olympiad streak of discus legend Al Oerter.

At 4 feet, 5 1/2 inches tall, 15-year-old Chinese gymnast Lu Li was the smallest competitor in the finals of the uneven bars at the 1992 Olympics. She won the gold medal by executing a flawless routine that earned 10s from all six judges.

I n a little more than 81 seconds of sheer speed and moves, Deborah Compagnoni left behind the field to win the gold medal in the super giant slalom in Albertville, France, in February 1992. Compagnoni also won gold medals in the giant slalom in the 1994 and 1998 Olympics.

B onnie Blair powers her way to gold in women's 1000-meter speed skating in 1992. Earlier, Blair had won the 500 meter for the second time. In 1994 she repeated her double gold-medal haul.

Michael Johnson, having easily defeated Frank Fredericks of Namibia and the other contenders, checks out his world record time (19.32) in the 200-meter run at the Atlanta Olympics in 1996. Johnson became the first man to win both the 200-meter and 400-meter races, setting an Olympic record of 43.49 in the longer event.

Sammy Sosa hit 66 home runs in 1998, breaking the old mark by five, but he played second fiddle to Mark McGwire.

On September 8, 1998, Mark McGwire stroked his 62nd home run of the season to break Roger Maris' 37-year-old record. With Sosa's own record pace spurring him on, the St. Louis first baseman went on to establish a new mark of 70.

Wor128orld champions! New York Yankees Chuck Knoblauch, Joe Girardi, and Mariano Rivera celebrate after sweeping San Diego to win the 1998 World Series.

Rickey Henderson celebrated in unusual fashion after recording his major league record 939th stolen base. Henderson broke Lou Brock's record by stealing third in a game against the Yankees.

Since his rookie year on the NASCAR circuit in 1993, Jeff Gordon has won the Daytona 500 twice, the Coca-Cola 600 three times, the Southern 500 four times, and the year-long Winston Cup driving championship three times. His first Daytona 500 victory in 1997 (above, car No. 24) made him the youngest winner of stock car racing's biggest event.

Credits

Allsport, all rights reserved: 238, 248 top

Allsport Historical Collection, all rights reserved: 142 bottom

Allsport USA, all rights reserved: 84

Allsport/Shan Butterill, all rights reserved: 241

Allsport/Simon Bruty, all rights reserved: 239 bottom

Allsport USA/Tony Duffy, all rights reserved: 162

Allsport/Bill Frakes, all rights reserved: 225

Allsport/Hulton Deutsch, all rights reserved: 97 bottom, 142 top

Allsport/Hulton Getty, all rights reserved: 86 bottom

Allsport/Jamie McDonald, all rights reserved: 239 top

Allsport/Adrian Murrell, all rights reserved: 208–209

Allsport/Steve Powell, all rights reserved: 206–207

Amateur Athletic Foundation: 47 right

Archive Photos/Popperfoto: 18, 22 (2), 72, 82–83, 88–89, 90 top, 91, 93, 131, 147, 159, 164, 186, 223 top, 250 top

Archive Photos/Reuters: Michael Probst: 229, 249

Archive Photos/Reuters: Nick Didlick: 224 top

Associated Press/Wide World Photos: 6 bottom right, 14–15, 24 bottom, 33 top, 41, 68, 69 (2), 70–71, 76 (2), 79, 80, 85, 92–93, 99, 102–103, 106–107, 107, 114, 115 bottom, 127, 138, 141, 143 (3), 154–155, 160 (2), 163 bottom, 171 bottom, 175 (2), 176 top, 180, 181, 184–185, 190 bottom, 193, 198–199, 221 bottom, 253 right

Associated Press/Wide World Photos: Reed Saxon: 204–205

Associated Press/Wide World Photos: Charles Arbogast: 235

Associated Press/Wide World Photos: John Bazemore: 254 top

Associated Press/Wide World Photos: Phil Coale: 254 bottom

Associated Press/Wide World Photos: Robert Dear: 218 bottom

Associated Press/Wide World Photos: Gary Dineen: 252 top

Associated Press/Wide World Photos: Ron Frehm: 230–231, 236

Associated Press/Wide World Photos: Wilbur Funches: 214 bottom

Associated Press/Wide World Photos: John Gaps III: 252 bottom

Associated Press/Wide World Photos: Lenny Ignelzi: 216 bottom, 221 top

Associated Press/Wide World Photos: Nils Meilvang: 244 top

Associated Press/Wide World Photos: David J. Phillip: 242 bottom

Associated Press/Wide World Photos: Rick Risberg: 216 top

Associated Press/Wide World Photos: Jack Smith: 230

Associated Press/Wide World Photos: Adam Stoltman: 218 (2)

J.M. Barey/Vandystadt (SI): 208

Robert Beck (SI): 7 bottom right, 233, 240, 242 top

John Biever (SI): 231, 253 left

Courtesy of Boston Herald, photo by Ray Cussier: 178–179

Brown Brothers: 6 bottom left, 21 bottom; 47 left, 63, 73 bottom, 78 (2), 87, 101 bottom

Chicago Historical Society: 52 top, 62 bottom

Gerry Cranham (SI): 169

College Football Hall of Fame: 40–41, 133

Corbis/Bettmann-UPI ©: Pat Benic: 213, 223 bottom

Corbis/Bettmann-UPI ©: Herb Scharfman: 150

Corbis/Bettmann-UPI ©: 5, 24 top, 27 top, 73 top, 74, 75 (2), 111, 132–133, 185, 217, 250 bottom

Corbis/Reuters ©: David Tulis: 243

Culver Pictures: 6 top left, 16–17, 17, 18–19, 21 top, 25 (3), 26, 27 bottom, 28 (2), 29, 30–31, 32 bottom, 34–35, 36–37, 39, 44 (2), 46 top, 49 (2), 54 (2), 55 (2), 56 top, 57 (2), 61, 77, 84–85, 86–87, 90 bottom, 97 top, 112 bottom, 115 top, 116–117, 117, 119, 122 bottom, 123, 124, 126 bottom

Cumberland County Historical Society: 46 bottom

Daytona Racing Archives: 134–135

James Drake (SI): 7 top right, 204

Nate Fine/NFL Photos: 113

Bill Frakes (SI): 2–3, 226–227

George Gellatly/NFL Photos: 145

Stephen Green/Armytage (SI): 198

John D. Hanlon (SI): 200

Hockey Hall of Fame: 62–63, 170

Hockey Hall of Fame/Imperial Oil–Turofsky: 7 top left, 139

John Iacono (SI): 187 top

Walter Iooss Jr. (SI): 1, 10–11, 167 bottom, 173, 202–203, 234, 248 bottom, 247 (2)

Mark Kauffman (SI): 148

Keeneland/Cook: 6 center left, 42 bottom

Heinz Kluetmeier (SI): 7 bottom left, 189, 196, 201, 222, 224 bottom, 250–251

David E. Klutho (SI): 214 top

Kyodo News Service: 237

Neil Leifer (SI): 7 center left, 157, 165, 174, 190 top, 191

Frank Lennon: 184

Library of Congress: 33 bottom, 67 bottom,

Richard Mackson (SI): 210, 232–233, 246

Bob Martin (SI): 232, 245

John W. McDonough (SI): 215

Manny Millan (SI): 195, 219

Peter Read Miller/NFL Photos: 197 bottom

Ronald C. Modra (SI): 207, 220 top

Bruce Murray Collection: 6 top right, 101 top

Naismith Memorial Basketball Hall of Fame, Springfield, MA: 125, 172, 194

Ancil Nance (SI): 211

National Baseball Library: 9, 13, 35, 52–53, 58–59, 98–99, 110, 120 (2), 132

National Cowboy Hall of Fame, Oklahoma City: 171 top

Dan Nerney (SI): 212

New York *Daily News:* 149

Oxford Daily Mail: 146

Hy Peskin (SI): 134 top, 140, 144 top, 151

Pittsburgh Post Gazette: Morris Berman: 166 bottom

Pro Football Hall of Fame/NFL Photos: 48, 94–95, 104, 109, 112 top, 134 bottom, 167 top, 180–181

Robert Riger/NFL Photos: 144 bottom

Herb Scharfman (SI): 187 bottom,

Scott Polar Research Institute: 32 top

George Silk/LIFE Magazine © Time Inc.: 6–7, 176–177

Damian Strohmeyer (SI): 244 bottom

Swimming Hall of Fame: 126 top

John Thorn: 40, 42 top, 182–183

Tony Triolo (SI): 188, 192,

Transcendental Graphics: 12, 20, 42 right, 50–51, 53 top, 56 bottom, 60–61, 62 top, 66 (2), 67 top, 83, 86 top, 100, 108–109, 118, 120–121, 122 top, 128–129, 130–131, 136, 137, 154

University of Southern California Sports Information Office: 96 top, 197 top

United States Golf Association: 43, 64–65

United States Olympic Committee: 23 (2), 110–111, 158–159, 163 top

Jerry Wachter (SI): 220 bottom

Western Reserve Historical Society: 38–39

Carl Yarbrough (SI): 228–229

John G. Zimmerman (SI): 152–153, 156–157, 161, 166 top, 168